# RUNNER'S WORLD

# MEALS
## *on the*
# RUN

# RUNNER'S WORLD
# MEALS
## *on the* RUN

### 150 energy-packed recipes in
### 30 MINUTES OR LESS

Edited by **Joanna Sayago Golub**

RODALE

Also by Joanna Sayago Golub

**The Runner's World Cookbook**

Mention of specific companies, organizations, or authorities in this book does not imply endorsement by the author or publisher, nor does mention of specific companies, organizations, or authorities imply that they endorse this book, its author, or the publisher.

Internet addresses and telephone numbers given in this book were accurate at the time it went to press.

Some of the recipes were previously published in *Runner's World* magazine and on runnersworld.com. For a full list of contributors, see page 242

© 2015 by Rodale, Inc.

Rodale books may be purchased for business or promotional use or for special sales. For information, please write to: Special Markets Department, Rodale Inc., 733 Third Avenue, New York, NY 10017.

Printed in the United States of America

Rodale Inc. makes every effort to use acid-free ♾, recycled paper ♻.

Book design by Christina Gaugler
Food photography by Mitch Mandel
Editor photo on page 249 by David E. Graf

Library of Congress Cataloging-in-Publication Data is on file with the publisher.

ISBN-13: 978-1-62336-583-7 trade hardcover

Distributed to the trade by Macmillan

2  4  6  8  10  9  7  5  3  1   hardcover

We inspire and enable people to improve their lives and the world around them.
rodalebooks.com

For my kids

# CONTENTS

# FOREWORD

As a runner, I care about what goes into my body. I want to know that I am fueling right, recovering properly, and gaining all the nutrition I can from my food. If I had the time, I'd study and research everything I ate—before it landed on my plate—and I wouldn't worry about how long it took to prepare my meals. But the truth is, sometimes I struggle to do it right. Not only am I a full-time professional athlete, but I am also a mother, a wife, and a business woman. To say that I am busy is an understatement: I start my day with work—meetings with sponsors, interviews for media—then go off to train for a few hours on the road or track. After that comes one of the best parts of my day—spending time with my son. Then it's back to training again. When I get home, it's a rush to get dinner on the table, clean up, and then get ready to do it all over again the next day. Sound familiar? Finding the time to make meals for my family can be tough and often feels overwhelming. I could use some help navigating the nutritional landscape—and I know I am not the only person in this situation. I'm sure that many of you feel the same way.

*Runner's World Meals on the Run* is a terrific resource for people like us. It's filled with recipes and information that will make you feel confident in the food choices you're making. Not only do all the recipes take just 30 minutes or less (we can all find time for that!), they also use natural and minimally processed ingredients—something that I care about greatly, since I am keenly aware that what you put into your body has a direct effect on your performance and health. As an athlete, I was drawn to the fact that all the nutrition information is broken down for each recipe, so you know exactly what nutrients you're getting. I find this especially helpful since I am always trying to make sure I get enough protein (to recover from those twice-a-day workouts) and fat (to help prevent injuries) in my diet.

Another helpful feature is the ribbon of tabs at the top of each page that categorizes recipes as vegetarian, low-calorie, recovery, and more. It lets you know what type of recipe it is at a quick glance, which is great for those of us who don't have time to read through each and every recipe. And perhaps my favorite thing about the book is the short explanation that proceeds each recipe; you learn why this particular recipe is important, what nutritional benefit you will gain from eating it, and when you should include it in your day. The amount of information in this cookbook is tremendous, and it's organized in an easy and useful manner. It is a bible of nutrition for runners with full lives—in essence, all of us!

Now when I'm making meal choices for myself and my family, I know I have the ultimate resource at my fingertips, allowing me to cook healthy, delicious, runner-friendly meals (in just 30 minutes!) that will also satisfy my family. We all lead busy lives, but with help from this cookbook, you can feel great about what you are putting into your body—while also making your life a little easier and less hectic along the way. Cheers!

*Kara Goucher*
*American marathoner and two-time Olympian*

# INTRODUCTION

Whether you are a brand new runner or experienced marathoner, all runners share one thing in common: We don't have a lot of time to spare in our day. Between responsibilities at work and home, most of us are busier than we like. Despite that fact, we carve out time in our hectic days to get out for a run—sometimes that means lacing up in the predawn hours, other times it means skipping a work lunch to squeeze in a couple miles. It's not easy to fit it in, but we do because running energizes our bodies and calms our minds. Without it, we know we would be worse off—both physically and mentally.

But runners also know you can't run well if you're not taking time to feed your body well. Just as we carve out an hour here or there for our workouts, we need to set aside time to prepare meals that will fuel our running. So how much time are we talking about? Less than you might think. If you've got 30 minutes, you can prepare fresh, delicious meals that will fuel your running and satisfy your appetite. Within the pages of this cookbook you'll find more than 150 recipes that help you do just that. From simple snacks and smoothies to weeknight dinners, you'll find everything you need to get food on the table fast. Need a hearty postrun breakfast but don't have time for a long-simmering oatmeal? Try our quick version with five different variations beginning on page 7. Searching for a fast dinner to fuel you up the night before your long run? Try one of the five pasta recipes featuring no-cook sauces, including Spaghetti with Sun-Dried Tomato Sauce (page 133).

Runners with special dietary needs will find plenty to choose from, too. If you follow a vegetarian, vegan, or gluten-free diet, simply scan the recipe tabs at the top of each page to see if a particular recipe fits your needs. If you're trying to lose weight, pay special attention to the recipes labeled Low-Calorie—there are more than 100, and they all have 400 calories or fewer per serving. You can also search the Special Recipe Lists beginning on page 231 to find all the recipes listed by dietary or performance need.

No matter which recipes appeal most to you, you'll quickly notice a common thread tying them together: They all feature fresh, minimally processed ingredients. Building your diet on wholesome, natural foods is a key tenet of our nutrition philosophy at *Runner's World*. These foods offer the best in terms of nutrition and taste—we believe that just because you only have 30 minutes to cook, you shouldn't have to compromise on either. That's also why every recipe in this book has gone through the rigors of the Rodale Test Kitchen. The result is a comprehensive collection of easy-to-follow recipes that fit within your busy lifestyle. Once you get cooking, we think you'll quickly agree that fast meals can be synonymous with good taste, good health, and good running.

Joanna Sayago Golub
Contributing Editor, *Runner's World*

# THE FAST RUNNER'S KITCHEN

The key to getting meals on the table quickly is starting with a fully stocked kitchen. That means keeping essential ingredients (both fresh and long-lasting) on hand and utilizing smart, timesaving tools. Here's everything you need to get cooking.

## PANTRY STAPLES

Keep your kitchen stocked with these essential ingredients. Most of them are familiar staples—but some may be new to you. Buy these unfamiliar ingredients once (almost all are readily available at most supermarkets) and you'll quickly see why they should be in every runner's kitchen.

### Canned Goods

**Anchovies and sardines**

**Beans (all varieties)**

**Chipotle peppers in adobo sauce**

**Coconut milk**

**Green chilies (chopped)**

**Pumpkin (not pumpkin pie mix)**

**Tomatoes (whole, chopped, diced, crushed, and paste)**

**Tuna**

**Wild salmon**

### Dried Fruits

**Apricots**

**Dates**

**Raisins**

**Tart cherries**

**Unsweetened blueberries**

**Unsweetened flaked coconut**

### Flavor Boosters

**Broth (chicken, beef, and vegetable)**

**Capers**

**Cocoa powder (unsweetened)**

**Dried herbs and spices**

Small but powerful, sardines are eco-friendly and rich in omega-3s.

Try your hand at making your own nut butters with the recipes on pages 62 to 64.

Canola oil is a good choice for very high-heat cooking.

Buy oil-packed sun-dried tomatoes. They're softer and more pliable than dried versions.

An ideal fuel source for runners, potatoes provide carbs, fiber, potassium, and vitamin C.

Pack a handful of raisins in a plastic zip-top bag and take them with you for midrun fuel.

Mustard

Pesto

Roasted red peppers

Sun-dried tomatoes

Sun-dried tomato spread

Tahini

Worcestershire sauce

## Frozen Foods

Corn

Edamame

Green beans (whole and cut)

Peas

Squash puree

Unsweetened fruits

Whole grain toaster waffles

Whole wheat pizza dough

## Long-Lasting Vegetables

Carrots

Celery

Potatoes (sweet, red, Yukon, and russet)

Garlic

Ginger

Onions

## Nuts and Seeds

Almonds (whole and sliced)

Cashews

Hazelnuts

Nut butters

Peanuts

Pecans

Pine nuts

Pumpkin seeds

Sunflower seeds

Walnuts

## Oils and Vinegars

Balsamic vinegar

Canola oil

Coconut oil

Extra-virgin olive oil

Red and white wine vinegar

Sherry vinegar

Specialty oils

## Pastas, Noodles, and Grains

Barley (quick-cooking)

Brown rice (10-minute varieties)

Bulgur

Oats (old-fashioned and steel-cut)

Pasta (short and long shapes)

Polenta (instant)

Quinoa

Rice noodles

Whole wheat couscous

Whole wheat orzo

Whole wheat panko breadcrumbs

Mustard is a low-calorie way to amp up flavor. Keep a variety on hand, including smooth Dijon, whole grain Dijon, and spicy brown.

Rice noodles cook faster than traditional Italian pastas.

Load up on store-bought frozen fruit, including mango, strawberries, blueberries, cherries, peaches, raspberries, and blackberries.

Celery will stay fresh in your refrigerator crisper for weeks.

Buy small bottles of walnut, avocado, and flaxseed oil for occasional use. Store in a dark, cool place.

Fresh garlic is much more flavorful than jarred and takes just a minute or two to prep.

## Sauces and Condiments (Asian)

They're worthy of their own section because they add distinct, powerful flavors.

**Curry paste (red and yellow)**

**Fish sauce**

**Hoison sauce**

**Kimchi**

**Miso**

**Oyster sauce**

**Red chili-garlic sauce (Sriracha)**

**Red chili paste**

**Rice vinegar**

**Soy sauce (regular and reduced-sodium)**

**Toasted (also called "dark") sesame oil**

## Sweeteners

All three have more nutrients than granulated sugar.

**Agave syrup (also called agave nectar)**

**Honey**

**Maple syrup**

Toasted sesame oil has an intense sesame flavor best used for drizzling over finished dishes.

Made with fermented cabbage, kimchi is rich in probiotic bacteria. Look for it in jars in the produce aisle.

# FRESH AND FAST PRODUCE

Yes, whole, fresh fruits and vegetables are the
healthiest, but when you're in a time-crunch,
already-prepared versions can speed things up with
minimal nutrient loss. Next time you're shopping,
give these smart shortcuts a try.

**Cleaned pomegranate seeds** Save yourself the
mess of cracking open a whole fruit and buy
a container of already cleaned seeds, rich in
inflammation-reducing antioxidants.

**Cubed melon** When you don't need (or have
room for) a whole watermelon, cantaloupe,
or honeydew melon, buy containers of
precubed and you'll waste less.

**Cut broccoli florets** Already trimmed from the
stalks, florets simply need a quick rinse and
they're ready for steaming.

**Peeled and cubed butternut squash** Just toss the
cubes with extra-virgin olive oil and roast in
the oven while prepping the rest of your meal.

**Prediced onion, celery, and carrot** Also called
"mirepoix," this diced vegetable mix is a great
shortcut when making soup.

**Prewashed greens** Salad greens come in an endless
number of mixes. Prewashed and chopped cooking
greens, like kale, spinach, and Swiss chard, make
it easy to cook these superfoods.

**Sliced mushrooms** Toss them into salads, stir-fries,
or omelets. Look for brands high in vitamin D for a
nutrient boost.

**Trimmed green beans** Snapping off tough ends is a
tedious task. Buy them already cleaned and save
yourself 10 minutes.

# TIME-SAVING TOOLS

You don't need any special equipment to cook the recipes in this book, but investing in a few kitchen tools can help save on prep time, as well as reduce the number of dirty pots and pans.

**Enameled cast-iron Dutch oven** This is true one-pot cooking. It can go from the stovetop to the oven and then straight to the table for serving. Cast-iron cookware retains heat incredibly well and can be used to cook soups and stews, as well as sear, brown, braise, or roast meat. Enameled versions are a breeze to clean, saving you time on the back-end, too. Buy one that is at least 5 quarts or, even better, 7 quarts (you don't need to fill the pot for it to work great).

**Garlic press** If a recipe calls for minced garlic, feel free to put it through a garlic press instead. It will save you a minute or two—and the results will taste infinitely better than garlic from a jar.

**Grater** Whether you need to grate cheese, carrots, ginger, or citrus zest, a stainless steel hand-held grater (such as a Microplane) gets the job done quickly.

**Immersion blender** Small and compact, an immersion blender allows you to puree soups without transferring them to a traditional blender—which saves you time and avoids dirtying up a larger, more cumbersome appliance. But be very careful when using; its blades are extremely sharp and it needs to be handled safely.

**Large chef's knife** This all-purpose knife makes quick work of chopping, dicing, and mincing vegetables of all sorts. Get one with an 8- to 9-inch blade. It may be larger than you need for some jobs but is far more versatile than a smaller blade.

**Stainless steel mixing bowls** You can easily find a nesting set of 6 bowls for less than $20. They take up little space in your cabinets and are endlessly useful when prepping or mixing ingredients. And unlike some fancier mixing bowls, they're dishwasher safe.

**Stainless steel skillet (12 inches)** This is the ideal skillet for almost every recipe in this book. Invest in a high-quality one and it will last forever. Unless you have an extra-large burner, skillets over 12 inches often heat unevenly and are cumbersome to handle. Nonstick skillets have their uses, but need to be replaced often, costing you more in the long run.

**Steamer basket** Steaming is one if the healthiest and easiest ways to cook vegetables. The basket fits inside a pot and sits above a few inches of boiling water. Cover with a lid, and veggies will be done in minutes.

# The Runner's Guide to PRERUN, MIDRUN, and POSTRUN FUEL

A s a runner, your most important food choices are what you eat before, during, and immediately after your run. So whether it's race morning and you're not sure what to eat, or you're in need of some appetizing midrun energy, or just want to make sure you properly kick-start your recovery, these recipes provide plenty of ways to meet your needs.

## PRERUN NUTRITION

Any runner who has had to wake up early for a race or long run knows how difficult it can be to eat well in the predawn hours. Many runners aren't hungry early in the morning and, if you're running a race, nerves can leave you feeling queasy. If you're staying at a hotel (without your go-to foods readily available) you run the risk of eating something that upsets your stomach. These quick breakfast ideas will fuel you up for a tough training run or race without weighing you down—and, if you pack a few ingredients, you can even make many of these meals in a hotel room, too.

**Almond-Cherry Granola (page 2)** Make a large batch of this granola ahead of time so you can grab a handful to snack on before your run. Eat it plain, mixed into oatmeal, or on "baked" apples, below.

**"Baked" Granola Apples (page 5)** If you've got a microwave in your hotel room (or in the hotel lobby), you can make this recipe. Halved, cooked apples get topped with sugar and cinnamon, plus granola for extra carbs.

**Chai Pumpkin Oatmeal (page 8)** This recipe uses a handy shortcut to get steel-cut oats on the table in just 15 minutes.

**Green Tea Smoothie (page 35)** Green tea provides caffeine for a performance boost, while kiwi, honeydew, and banana offer energizing carbs.

**Gingered Winter Greens Smoothie (page 40)** Fresh ginger may help calm a queasy stomach, while coconut water provides much needed electrolytes and will help hydrate you.

**Good Morning Sweet Potato (page 27)** Sweet potatoes provide quickly digested carbs for a satisfying energy boost. Just microwave the potato for 5 to 10 minutes and add maple syrup and walnuts.

## MIDRUN FUEL

Any time you run longer than an hour, you should pack some easily transportable fuel to power you through your workout. Energy gels and chews are a convenient choice, but sometimes you want something more substantial—and satisfying. These energy bars and balls are quick to make, really delicious, and will power you up during your workout.

**Honey Energy Bars (page 50)** Honey provides simple sugars (fructose and glucose), which are quickly absorbed and offer immediate energy.

**PackFit Bars (page 51)** These sweet and chewy bars contain dried tart cherries, which reduce inflammation that can lead to muscle soreness.

**Chocolate Chip Trail Mix Balls (page 55)** Salty and sweet, these tasty little snacks pack nuts, dried fruit, and, yes, chocolate, into an easily portable package.

# The Night Before

Fuel up the night before your long run or big race with one of these carb-rich meals:

**Spaghetti with Sun-Dried Tomato Sauce** (page 133)

**Pizza Margherita with Make-Ahead Tomato Sauce** (page 154)

**Soba Noodles with Peanut-Sesame Sauce** (page 131)

**Pasta with Peas and Prosciutto** (page 143)

**Kara Goucher's Kitchen Sink Pizza** (page 222)

**Spaghetti Carbonara** (page 147)

# POSTRUN RECOVERY

After a tough morning run or race, it's key to refuel with a combination of both carbohydrates, which will replenish muscle glycogen, and protein to repair and rebuild muscle tissue. But that recovery doesn't happen after just one meal. You need to continue to eat recovery-friendly foods throughout the day. Here's how to fuel up after a morning run to ensure your muscles are ready to go the next day.

## Breakfast

**"Eggy" Tofu Scramble (page 15)** Sautéed tofu with spices provides a high-protein alternative to traditional scrambled eggs.

**Blueberries 'n' Cream Oatmeal (page 12)** A creamy Greek yogurt topping bumps up the protein in this carb-packed meal.

**Southwestern Black Bean Wrap (page 21)** Black beans and brown rice are a classic carb-and-protein duo.

## Lunch

**Black and White Bean Sausage Soup (page 114)** Just a half-pound of sausage creates a meaty-tasting soup with plenty of protein. Beans provide a few extra grams of protein, plus carbs.

**Vietnamese-Style Pulled Chicken Sandwiches (page 226)** Made with rotisserie chicken, this quick, protein-packed sandwich is ideal for a make-ahead lunch.

## Dinner

**Lettuce-Wrapped Asian Salmon Burgers (page 193)** Salmon is a rich source of both protein and inflammation-reducing omega-3 fatty acids.

**Steak and Pepper Rice Bowl (page 211)** This all-in-one meal provides protein-rich beef, whole grain complex carbs, and antioxidant-packed vegetables.

**Tofu Peanut Stir-Fry (page 170)** Tofu provides protein, as well as isoflavones that may promote heart health.

# GUIDE TO THE RECIPE KEY

At the top of each recipe, you'll find our color-coded Recipe Key. This key lets you know if the recipe meets certain training goals or dietary needs. The definitions below explain the key in detail.

## PRERUN

Recipes marked Prerun supply the nutrients needed to fuel a run and can be eaten about 2 hours before a workout. The majority of calories in these recipes come from carbohydrates—your body's preferred source of energy. These recipes also contain fewer than about 10 grams of fat, 20 grams of protein, and about 7 grams of fiber or fewer per serving. Fat, protein, and fiber slow digestion and, for many runners, can cause an upset stomach if consumed too close to running. There are many other recipes in the cookbook not marked Prerun because they may fall slightly outside of these guidelines; some runners may have no problem eating these meals before a run. Because every runner has different tolerances, you should experiment to see what works for you. Remember to try any new foods long before an important race to ensure it won't upset your stomach.

## RECOVERY

Recipes marked Recovery are high in protein to repair muscle tissue and provide a dose of carbohydrates to restock your energy stores postrun. In general, optimal Recovery meals contain carbohydrates and protein in a ratio between 2:1 and 4:1 (carbohydrates to protein), with at least 15 grams of protein. Some recipes labeled Recovery may contain slightly fewer or more carbohydrates than the suggested ratio. Regardless of the amount of carbohydrates a recipe contains, meals can also earn the Recovery label if they provide 15 to 25 grams of protein per serving. Fat and fiber content are not taken into consideration, since they do not significantly affect recovery.

## VEGETARIAN

Recipes marked Vegetarian contain no meat, poultry, or fish. They may contain eggs, dairy, and honey.

## VEGAN

Recipes categorized as Vegan contain no animal products at all. These dishes are all vegetarian and additionally exclude eggs, dairy, and honey.

## LOW-CALORIE

This category is provided for runners who may be trying to lose weight or maintain a healthy weight. These recipes contain 400 calories or fewer per serving—or 20 percent of your total daily calorie needs based on a 2,000-calorie daily diet.

## 5-MINUTE FIX
## 10 MINUTES TOPS

These ultra quick recipes take just 5 minutes or 10 minutes, respectively, to prepare.

## GLUTEN-FREE

Recipes marked Gluten-Free contain no gluten, a protein found in wheat, barley, and rye. Many of these recipes use naturally gluten-free products, including chicken, beef, and vegetable broths; gluten-free grains, such as corn, rice, quinoa, and oats; and spices or spice blends. Because even naturally gluten-free products can sometimes be contaminated with trace amounts of gluten, it's key that runners who have an extreme sensitivity check product labels. Bob's Red Mill offers an extensive line of grains and flours certified gluten-free, while broths made by Pacific Foods, Imagine Foods, and Kitchen Basics are gluten-free. Bottled and jarred condiments (such as soy sauce) that typically contain gluten are not used in the Gluten-Free recipes. Many of these products are available in gluten-free versions and can be substituted for the traditional product.

## HYDRATING

Staying hydrated is key when it comes to optimizing performance, health, and well-being. Recipes that are labeled Hydrating contain a large amount of fluid from liquid ingredients or foods that are naturally high in water, such as fruits and vegetables. In addition to providing fluids, Hydrating recipes contain a blend of key electrolytes, including sodium and potassium, which are lost in sweat.

# BREAKFAST

## *Granola and Hot Cereal*

## *Eggs, Pancakes, and Sweet Starts*

# ALMOND-CHERRY GRANOLA

**Recipe by THE RODALE TEST KITCHEN**

**MAKES 5 CUPS**
**TOTAL TIME: 20 MINUTES,**
**PLUS COOLING TIME**

6 tablespoons canola oil

2 tablespoons agave syrup or honey

¼ cup maple syrup

½ teaspoon vanilla extract

¼ teaspoon almond extract

2 cups old-fashioned rolled oats

½ cup slivered almonds

¼ cup chopped cashews

½ cup toasted wheat germ

½ teaspoon ground cinnamon

⅛ teaspoon ground cloves

½ cup dried tart cherries

*Made with whole grains, nuts, and dried fruit, granola packs runner-friendly nutrients, including carbs, fiber, healthy fats, and antioxidants. Paired with yogurt, it's a quick, satisfying breakfast.*

Preheat the oven to 350°F.

In a medium bowl, stir together the oil, agave syrup, maple syrup, vanilla, and almond extract. In a large bowl, combine the oats, almonds, cashews, wheat germ, cinnamon, and cloves. Pour the oil mixture over the oat mixture and stir to combine, making sure the dry ingredients are well coated.

Spread the granola on a rimmed baking sheet. Bake for 15 minutes, stirring occasionally, until the granola turns golden brown. Remove from the oven. Sprinkle the cherries over the granola and allow the granola to cool on the pan before storing in an airtight container for up to 3 weeks.

NUTRITION PER ¼ CUP: 130 calories, 15 g carbs, 2 g fiber, 3 g protein, 7 g total fat, 0.5 g saturated fat, 0 mg sodium

QUICK TIP Make a big batch of this granola and use it in any of the following recipes that call for granola as an ingredient.

# "BAKED" GRANOLA APPLES

Recipe by THE RODALE TEST KITCHEN

**MAKES 4 SERVINGS**
**TOTAL TIME: 10 MINUTES**

- 2 large crisp apples, such as Gala, halved and cored
- 2 tablespoons chopped dried tart cherries
- 1 tablespoon packed light brown sugar
- ¼ teaspoon ground cinnamon
- ⅛ teaspoon ground nutmeg
- 4 teaspoons butter
- ½ cup granola, such as Almond-Cherry Granola (page 2)

*The secret behind getting these "baked" apples on the table fast? Cooking them in the microwave, which quickly steams the fruit until perfectly tender. Use a spoon or melon baller to core the halved apples. Top the finished dish with a dollop of yogurt for a protein and calcium boost.*

In a microwavable dish, arrange the apple halves cut side up.

Top each apple half evenly with the tart cherries and brown sugar. Sprinkle with the cinnamon and nutmeg. Dot evenly with the butter.

Cover the apples with a microwavable dome lid. Microwave on high for about 4 minutes, or until the apples are tender.

Transfer the apples to serving bowls and sprinkle each apple half evenly with the granola. Drizzle any juices remaining in the cooking dish over the top.

**NUTRITION PER SERVING:** 185 calories, 29 g carbs, 5 g fiber, 2 g protein, 8 g total fat, 2.5 g saturated fat, 36 mg sodium

**QUICK TIP** Braeburn, Cortland, or Rome apples work just as well as Gala.

# CHOCOLATE-BANANA GRANOLA BOWLS

Recipe by MATTHEW KADEY, M.S., R.D.

**MAKES 2 SERVINGS**
**TOTAL TIME: 10 MINUTES**

1 cup 2% plain Greek yogurt

2 bananas, frozen

2 tablespoons unsalted natural-style peanut butter

2 tablespoons unsweetened cocoa powder

1 tablespoon honey

1 teaspoon vanilla extract

½ teaspoon ground cinnamon

⅔ cup granola, such as Almond-Cherry Granola (page 2)

*Swap out your usual yogurt-and-granola breakfast for this power-packed upgrade that blends thick and creamy Greek yogurt with frozen bananas. The fruit adds energizing carbs, potassium, and vitamin B₆, a nutrient that bolsters brain functioning. Greek yogurt has about twice the protein of regular yogurt and will give you sustained energy all morning.*

In a blender, combine the yogurt, bananas, peanut butter, cocoa powder, honey, vanilla, and cinnamon. Blend until smooth.

Divide between 2 bowls and top with the granola.

NUTRITION PER SERVING: 491 calories, 64 g carbs, 9 g fiber, 21 g protein, 19 g total fat, 3.5 g saturated fat, 50 mg sodium

**QUICK TIP** Don't toss those overripe bananas sitting on your kitchen counter. Peel them and freeze in plastic bags, so you can use them in this recipe, as well as in smoothies.

# QUICK-COOKING STEEL-CUT OATMEAL

Recipe by MATTHEW KADEY, M.S., R.D.

**MAKES 4 SERVINGS**
**TOTAL TIME: 15 MINUTES,**
**PLUS SOAKING OVERNIGHT**

1 cup steel-cut oats
2½ cups filtered water
Pinch of salt

*Steel-cut oatmeal has a chewy, hearty texture and rich, nutty flavor that more processed oats can't match. It is also lower on the glycemic index than other types of oats, which means it helps keep your blood sugar at a steady level. Problem is, it can take longer than 30 minutes to get a bowl of steel-cut oatmeal from the canister to the table. But there's a shortcut: By lightly simmering and then soaking the oats overnight, you only need to cook them for about 10 minutes the following morning (even less if you microwave them). Once the oats are cooked, add your favorite toppings, or try one of the five flavored oatmeal recipes that follow.*

In a medium saucepan, combine the oats, water, and salt. Bring to a slight simmer over high heat, then continue to simmer for 1 minute. The surface should be foamy and cloudy but not yet boiling. Cover, then remove from the heat. Let the oats soak unrefrigerated overnight.

In the morning, put the saucepan over medium-low heat and cook, stirring occasionally, for about 12 minutes, or until the oats are creamy and of desired consistency. (Alternatively, transfer the oats and liquid to a large microwavable bowl, cover, and microwave on high in 30-second increments for about 3 minutes, or until creamy.)

**NUTRITION PER SERVING:** 140 calories, 27 g carbs, 4 g fiber, 6 g protein, 3 g total fat, 0.5 g saturated fat, 42 mg sodium

# CHAI PUMPKIN OATMEAL

Recipe by MATTHEW KADEY, M.S., R.D.

**MAKES 4 SERVINGS**
**TOTAL TIME: 15 MINUTES**

> 1 cup steel-cut oats, soaked overnight (see page 7)
>
> ¼ cup 2% milk
>
> ½ cup canned unsweetened pumpkin puree
>
> 1 teaspoon vanilla extract
>
> ½ teaspoon ground cinnamon
>
> ½ teaspoon ground ginger
>
> ¼ teaspoon ground nutmeg
>
> ⅛ teaspoon ground cloves
>
> ¼ cup chopped pecans or walnuts
>
> ¼ cup unsweetened flaked coconut
>
> 2 tablespoons plus 2 teaspoons maple syrup

*Canned pumpkin provides natural sweetness and a hefty dose of beta-carotene, an antioxidant used by the body to make vitamin A, which bolsters immune and eye health. Real maple syrup, particularly darker grades, is a surprising source of antioxidant firepower.*

After soaking the oats overnight, place the saucepan over medium-low heat and cook, stirring occasionally, for about 12 minutes, or until the oats are creamy and of desired consistency. (Alternatively, transfer the oats and liquid to a large microwavable bowl. Cover and microwave on high in 30-second increments for about 3 minutes, or until creamy.)

When the oats are cooked, add the milk, pumpkin puree, vanilla, cinnamon, ginger, nutmeg, and cloves. Stir until well combined and heated through.

Divide the oatmeal among 4 bowls. Top each serving with 1 tablespoon pecans, 1 tablespoon coconut, and 2 teaspoons maple syrup.

NUTRITION PER SERVING: 285 calories, 42 g carbs, 7 g fiber, 8 g protein, 12 g total fat, 4.5 g saturated fat, 54 mg sodium

**QUICK TIP** You can also make this recipe (and all the flavored oatmeal recipes in this chapter) using old-fashioned rolled oats in place of steel-cut: Add 2 cups old-fashioned rolled oats to 3¾ cups boiling water. Cook according to the package directions.

# GREEN EGGS AND HAM OATMEAL

Recipe by MATTHEW KADEY, M.S., R.D.

**MAKES 4 SERVINGS**
**TOTAL TIME: 15 MINUTES**

- 1 cup steel-cut oats, soaked overnight (see page 7)
- 2 teaspoons extra-virgin olive oil
- 4 large eggs
- ⅓ cup low-sodium chicken or vegetable broth
- 3 cups baby spinach
- ⅓ cup grated Parmesan cheese
- ⅓ cup chopped oil-packed sun-dried tomatoes
- ¼ teaspoon ground black pepper
- 4 ounces Black Forest ham, chopped
- 4 teaspoons chopped fresh chives
- Hot sauce, for serving (optional)

*Delicious for breakfast, this savory oatmeal tastes just as great for lunch or even dinner. Lean ham and eggs deliver protein to help keep hunger at bay. Spinach contains nitrates that are shown to improve muscle functioning during exercise.*

After soaking the oats overnight, place the saucepan over medium-low heat and cook, stirring occasionally, for about 12 minutes, or until the oats are creamy and of desired consistency. (Alternatively, transfer the oats and liquid to a large microwavable bowl. Cover and microwave on high in 30-second increments for about 3 minutes, or until creamy.)

Meanwhile, in a large skillet, heat the oil over medium heat. Add the eggs and fry until the edges of the whites are set, about 1 minute. For sunny side up, cover and cook for 3 to 5 minutes longer, depending on desired doneness. For over-easy, flip eggs instead of covering, and cook until desired doneness. Transfer eggs to a plate and cover to keep warm.

When the oats are cooked, add the broth, spinach, Parmesan, sun-dried tomatoes, and pepper. Stir until the spinach wilts and the mixture is heated through.

Divide the oatmeal among 4 bowls. Top each serving with 1 ounce of the ham, 1 fried egg, 1 teaspoon chives, and a couple dashes of hot sauce, if desired.

NUTRITION PER SERVING: 340 calories, 32 g carbs, 5 g fiber, 21 g protein, 16 g total fat, 4.5 g saturated fat, 476 mg sodium

Quick-Cooking Steel-Cut
Oatmeal, page 7

Bacon-Apple-Chedder
Oatmeal, page 14

Tropical Twister
Oatmeal, page 13

Chai Pumpkin Oatmeal,
page 8

Green Eggs and Ham
Oatmeal, page 9

Blueberries 'n' Cream
Oatmeal, page 12

# BLUEBERRIES 'N' CREAM OATMEAL

### Recipe by MATTHEW KADEY, M.S., R.D.

**MAKES 4 SERVINGS**
**TOTAL TIME: 15 MINUTES**

1 cup steel-cut oats, soaked overnight (see page 7)

⅓ cup 2% milk

1 cup blueberries

1 teaspoon grated lemon zest

1 teaspoon ground allspice

½ teaspoon almond extract (optional)

1⅓ cups 2% plain Greek yogurt

¼ cup chopped almonds

4 teaspoons honey

*Blueberries contain more flavonoid antioxidants, which work to fortify heart health, than almost any other fruit. Choose organic versions when you can—studies show they contain significantly higher concentrations of those beneficial antioxidants than conventionally grown varieties.*

After soaking the oats overnight, place the saucepan over medium-low heat and cook, stirring occasionally, for about 12 minutes, or until the oats are creamy and of desired consistency. (Alternatively, transfer the oats and liquid to a large microwavable bowl. Cover and microwave on high in 30-second increments for about 3 minutes, or until creamy.)

When the oats are cooked, add the milk, blueberries, lemon zest, allspice, and almond extract (if using). Stir until well combined and heated through.

Divide the oatmeal among 4 bowls. Top each serving with ⅓ cup yogurt, 1 tablespoon almonds, and 1 teaspoon honey.

NUTRITION PER SERVING: 298 calories, 44 g carbs, 6 g fiber, 17 g protein, 8 g total fat, 2.5 g saturated fat, 81 mg sodium

# TROPICAL TWISTER OATMEAL

Recipe by MATTHEW KADEY, M.S., R.D.

**MAKES 4 SERVINGS**
**TOTAL TIME: 15 MINUTES**

- 1 cup steel-cut oats, soaked overnight (see page 7)
- ⅓ cup canned coconut milk
- 2 tablespoons packed light brown sugar or coconut sugar
- 1 teaspoon grated fresh ginger
- 1 teaspoon vanilla extract
- ¼ teaspoon ground cardamom
- 2 cups chopped mango (about 2 mangoes)
- ¼ cup chopped pistachios
- ¼ cup cacao nibs

*A splash of coconut milk adds creamy sweetness, while mango packs plenty of vitamin C, which can help lower blood pressure. Cacao nibs have great chocolaty crunch and good amounts of dietary fiber to keep you feeling full all morning long.*

After soaking the oats overnight, place the saucepan over medium-low heat and cook, stirring occasionally, for about 12 minutes, or until the oats are creamy and of desired consistency. (Alternatively, transfer the oats and liquid to a large microwavable bowl. Cover and microwave on high in 30-second increments for about 3 minutes, or until creamy.)

When the oats are cooked, add the coconut milk, brown sugar, ginger, vanilla, and cardamom. Stir until well combined and heated through.

Divide the oatmeal among 4 bowls. Top each serving with ½ cup mango, 1 tablespoon pistachios, and 1 tablespoon cacao nibs.

NUTRITION PER SERVING: 339 calories, 53 g carbs, 9 g fiber, 9 g protein, 13 g total fat, 5.5 g saturated fat, 81 mg sodium

**QUICK TIP** You can substitute frozen mango if you can't find fresh. Just defrost in the microwave before using.

# BACON-APPLE-CHEDDAR OATMEAL

Recipe by MATTHEW KADEY, M.S., R.D.

**MAKES 4 SERVINGS**
**TOTAL TIME: 15 MINUTES**

1 cup steel-cut oats, soaked overnight (see page 7)

4 slices bacon

⅓ cup water

1 apple, chopped

3 tablespoons maple syrup

1 cup shredded cheddar cheese

¼ cup chopped walnuts

*Bacon and apples collide in this sweet and savory bowl. Cheddar cheese provides a dose of bone-building calcium, while research shows polyphenol antioxidants in apples can help lower cholesterol. Among nuts, walnuts lead the way in heart-healthy omega-3 fats.*

After soaking the oats overnight, place the saucepan over medium-low heat and cook, stirring occasionally, for about 12 minutes, or until the oats are creamy and of desired consistency. (Alternatively, transfer the oats and liquid to a large microwavable bowl. Cover and microwave on high in 30-second increments for about 3 minutes, or until creamy.)

Meanwhile, place the bacon in a large skillet and place over medium-low heat. Cook, turning frequently so that both sides cook evenly, until nearly crispy, 5 to 8 minutes total. Transfer to a plate lined with paper towels.

When the oats are cooked, add the water, apple, and syrup. Stir until well combined and heated through.

Divide the oatmeal among 4 bowls. Top each serving with ¼ cup cheddar and 1 tablespoon chopped walnuts. Crumble 1 slice of bacon over each bowl and serve.

NUTRITION PER SERVING: 408 calories, 45 g carbs, 6 g fiber, 17 g protein, 20 g total fat, 8 g saturated fat, 358 mg sodium

# "EGGY" TOFU SCRAMBLE

**Recipe by AMY FRITCH**

**MAKES 2 SERVINGS**
**TOTAL TIME: 20 MINUTES**

- 2 teaspoons ground cumin
- ½ teaspoon turmeric
- Pinch of chili powder (optional)
- ½ teaspoon salt
- ¼ teaspoon ground black pepper
- 3 tablespoons water
- 2 tablespoons canola oil
- 1 small onion, chopped
- 3 cloves garlic, minced
- 1 package (14 to 16 ounces) firm tofu, drained and crumbled into bite-size pieces
- 3 tablespoons nutritional yeast

*For vegan runners—or runners who just need a break from their morning egg routine—scrambled tofu is an excellent breakfast. Tofu provides quality protein and acts as a blank slate for whatever spices and flavorings you'd like to add. Here it takes on a rich, savory flavor thanks to the addition of nutritional yeast, which (if you're not yet familiar with it) is a staple in vegan diets and well worth a try. Look for it in the natural foods section of supermarkets or in health food stores. Vegans should choose brands fortified with vitamin $B_{12}$, since this nutrient is most abundant in animal sources, such as chicken and eggs.*

In a small bowl, combine the cumin, turmeric, chili powder (if using), salt, pepper, and water. Stir well. Set aside.

In a large skillet, heat the oil over medium-high heat. Add the onion and garlic and cook for 2 to 3 minutes, or until soft. Add the tofu and cook for 10 minutes, stirring often with a metal spatula so the tofu doesn't stick to the pan.

Add the spice mixture and nutritional yeast and stir gently to combine. If the pan is too dry, add a few teaspoons of water. Cook for 1 to 2 minutes more. Serve warm.

NUTRITION PER SERVING: 354 calories, 14 g carbs, 6 g fiber, 25 g protein, 23 g total fat, 3 g saturated fat, 600 mg sodium

**QUICK TIP** Toss in any leftover cooked vegetables you have on hand into the scramble for a nutrient boost.

# SIMPLE (OR STUFFED!) OMELETS

**Recipe by THE RODALE TEST KITCHEN**

**MAKES 2 SERVINGS**
**TOTAL TIME: 10 MINUTES**

1 tablespoon butter

4 large eggs

Pinch of salt

Pinch of ground white pepper

Fillings of choice (page 18)

*High in protein and rich in antioxidants, eggs should be a go-to food for runners. This no-fail omelet recipe showcases eggs at their best—and it's as delicious as it is simple. Classic French omelets are a bit creamy and wet on the inside. This recipe allows you to customize your omelet toward either a classic or more cooked style. Add any of the filling combinations listed on the next pages to make this a recovery-friendly meal. Just spread the filling on one side of the omelet before folding in half.*

Heat an 8-inch skillet over medium heat. Add half the butter and swirl until melted and foamy. The skillet should be very hot before the eggs are added.

In a large bowl, whisk the eggs until fully blended. Whisk in the salt and pepper.

Pour half the egg mixture into the hot pan. When the underside is set (after 30 to 45 seconds), continuously lift the edges of the omelet slightly with a fork or spatula and tilt the pan to let the uncooked egg flow underneath. Work your way around the pan in this manner for about 1 minute more.

As soon as the mixture appears set but is still soft and slightly wet, add any fillings, fold the omelet in half, and slide out onto a plate. For an omelet that's a little less wet and more set, before adding the fillings, cover the skillet and keep over the heat for another 30 seconds, or until the egg reaches desired doneness. Add any fillings, fold the omelet in half, and slide onto a plate.

Wipe the skillet clean with a paper towel and repeat with the remaining butter, egg mixture, and fillings.

NUTRITION PER SERVING (WITHOUT FILLING): 194 calories, 1 g carbs, 0 g fiber, 13 g protein, 15 g total fat, 7 g saturated fat, 265 mg sodium

# Fillings for Stuffed Omelets

Spread any of the following ingredients on one side of the omelet (see page 16) before folding. All fillings should be cooked and warmed, when appropriate.

**Apple Pie** ¼ cup diced apple sautéed in 1 teaspoon butter; 1 tablespoon shredded cheddar

**Bacon Bits** 1 slice cooked bacon, crumbled; ¼ avocado, sliced

**Blue Morning** 2 tablespoons bleu cheese, 2 tablespoons caramelized onions

**Carbonara** 2 tablespoons cooked diced pancetta, 2 tablespoons green peas, sprinkle of Parmesan

**Cheesy Broccoli** ¼ cup small broccoli florets, steamed; 1 tablespoon shredded Gruyère cheese

**Crab Cakes** ¼ cup shredded cooked crab; ½ teaspoon grated lemon zest; 1 scallion, chopped

**Curry Love** ¼ cup sautéed cubed tofu, ¼ teaspoon curry powder

**French Style** 2 tablespoons mixed fresh herbs, such as chives, tarragon, chervil, and parsley; 2 tablespoons soft goat cheese

**Greek** Small handful baby spinach, 1 tablespoon crumbled feta, 1 tablespoon diced tomato, 1 tablespoon chopped olives

**Green Eggs** 2 teaspoons pesto, small handful fresh arugula

**Grill Fest** ¼ cup leftover mixed grilled vegetables (eggplant, zucchini, yellow squash, bell pepper, onion)

**Guac and Roll** ¼ cup cooked corn, 1 tablespoon guacamole

**Hot Stuff** 3 tablespoons canned spicy black beans; ½ small jalapeño, sliced; dash of hot sauce

**Italian Feast** ¼ cup shredded mozzarella; 5 cherry tomatoes, halved; 4 large basil leaves, torn

**Korean Eggs** ¼ cup sautéed sliced zucchini; 2 tablespoons chopped kimchi; ½ scallion, chopped

**Lean Machine** ¼ cup diced cooked chicken or turkey, small handful fresh baby spinach

**Lox of Love** ¼ cup flaked smoked salmon, 1 tablespoon cream cheese, 1 tablespoon chopped chives

**Matzo Mash** ¼ cup crumbled matzo crackers, soaked in warm water; ¼ teaspoon ground cinnamon

**Meaty Start** 1 cooked breakfast sausage link, sliced; 1 slice cooked turkey bacon, crumbled

**Mex Eggs** 2 tablespoons salsa, 1 tablespoon queso fresco, 1 tablespoon fresh cilantro

**Pasta Perfect** ¼ cup leftover cooked elbow pasta; ½ tablespoon sun-dried tomato spread

**Protein Boost** 2 tablespoons Greek yogurt, 1 tablespoon pomegranate seeds, 1 teaspoon honey

**Spanish** ¼ cup sautéed diced potato, 2 tablespoons sautéed chopped yellow onion

**Spring Mix** ¼ cup cooked chopped asparagus, ½ tablespoon grated Parmesan cheese

**Steak and Eggs** ¼ cup leftover cooked, chopped steak; 2 tablespoons sautéed sliced mushrooms

**Sweet and Savory** ¼ cup crumbled feta cheese, 1 tablespoon diced dried apricots

**Western** ¼ cup mixed diced bell pepper and tomato, 1 tablespoon diced ham, 1 tablespoon shredded cheddar

# SOUTHWESTERN BLACK BEAN WRAP

**Recipe by AMY GORIN**

**MAKES 1 SERVING**
**TOTAL TIME: 15 MINUTES**

- 1 whole wheat tortilla (8 inches)
- 2 teaspoons canola oil
- ¼ cup canned black beans, drained and rinsed
- ¼ cup cooked brown rice
- ½ cup baby spinach
- 1 large egg, beaten
- 2 tablespoons shredded cheddar cheese
- ¼ avocado, sliced
- 2 tablespoons salsa
- 1 tablespoon chopped fresh cilantro

*For runners, beans are a perfect food—high in both protein and carbs, which makes them ideal for muscle recovery. Brown rice is a good source of manganese, a mineral that helps convert carbohydrates into energy.*

Heat a medium skillet over medium heat. Place the tortilla in the skillet and allow to warm for 1 minute. Flip and warm for 1 minute longer. Transfer to a plate.

Add 1 teaspoon of the oil to the skillet and swirl to coat the bottom. Add the beans, rice, and spinach. Cook for 2 minutes, stirring frequently, or until the beans and rice are warmed through and the spinach begins to wilt. Spread the mixture on one half of the tortilla.

Add the remaining 1 teaspoon oil to the skillet and swirl to coat the bottom. Add the egg and cook until scrambled. Transfer to the tortilla.

Top the tortilla with the cheese, avocado, salsa, and cilantro. Fold up both sides of the tortilla, then roll it up, slice in half, and serve.

NUTRITION PER SERVING: 524 calories, 51 g carbs, 11 g fiber, 20 g protein, 28 g total fat, 7 g saturated fat, 727 mg sodium

QUICK TIP This recipe is a great way to use up leftover brown rice. Or prepare a cup of 10-minute whole grain brown rice (which takes about 10 minutes to cook) according to the package directions.

# PUMPKIN-RICOTTA WAFFLES

Recipe by AMY GORIN

**MAKES 1 SERVING**
**TOTAL TIME: 5 MINUTES**

- 2 whole grain toaster waffles
- ¼ cup canned unsweetened pumpkin puree
- 2 tablespoons ricotta cheese
- 1 tablespoon maple syrup
- ⅛ teaspoon pumpkin pie spice
- 1 tablespoon chopped pecans

*Whole grain toaster waffles will keep you fuller longer than those made with refined grains thanks to the extra fiber. If you have the time, make 2 homemade waffles using 1 batch of dry Multigrain Buttermilk Pancake Mix (opposite) combined with ⅓ cup cold water, 1 egg, and 2 teaspoons canola oil; follow the manufacturer's directions on your waffle maker.*

Cook the waffles in a toaster.

Meanwhile, in a microwavable bowl, stir together the pumpkin, ricotta, maple syrup, and pumpkin pie spice until thoroughly combined. Heat in the microwave for 30 seconds, or until warmed through.

Spread the pumpkin mixture on the toasted waffles. Sprinkle with the pecans.

NUTRITION PER SERVING: 383 calories, 46 g carbs, 5 g fiber, 12 g protein, 18 g total fat, 5 g saturated fat, 295 mg sodium

# MULTIGRAIN BUTTERMILK PANCAKE MIX

Recipe by THE RODALE TEST KITCHEN

**MAKES 5 CUPS (ENOUGH FOR
5 BATCHES/4 PANCAKES EACH)
TOTAL TIME: 10 MINUTES**

### Pancake Mix

- ¾ cup ground flaxseeds
- 1½ cups whole wheat flour
- 1½ cups brown rice flour,
  oat flour, or sorghum flour
- ½ cup toasted wheat germ
- ½ cup buttermilk powder
- 2 tablespoons light brown
  sugar
- 4 teaspoons baking powder
- 1 teaspoon baking soda
- 1 teaspoon salt

### Pancakes

- 1 cup Multigrain Buttermilk
  Pancake Mix
- 1 large egg
- ⅔ cup cold water
- 3 teaspoons canola oil

*While store-bought pancake mixes are convenient, they often contain
unhealthy fats and rarely taste great. That's where this recipe comes in.
Keep a batch of this whole grain mix on hand, so all you have to do is add
the wet ingredients when you're ready.*

Make the pancake mix: In a large bowl, whisk together the ground
flaxseeds, whole wheat flour, brown rice flour, wheat germ, buttermilk powder, brown sugar, baking powder, baking soda, and salt.
Store, tightly sealed, in the refrigerator for several months.

To make pancakes (about 4): Measure the pancake mix into a large
bowl and make a well in the center. Stir in the egg, water, and 2 teaspoons of the canola oil.

Heat a large skillet or griddle over medium heat. Coat with the
remaining 1 teaspoon canola oil. For each pancake, ladle ⅓ cup
batter onto the skillet and cook for 2 to 3 minutes, or until the sides
bubble and the underside is browned. Flip and cook 1 to 2 minutes
longer, or until cooked through.

NUTRITION PER SERVING (2 PANCAKES): 329 calories, 43 g carbs, 7 g fiber,
12 g protein, 13 g total fat, 2 g saturated fat, 625 mg sodium

**QUICK TIP** Buttermilk powder is available in the baking section of
many supermarkets and from stores that specialize in baking supplies. You can also substitute dry milk powder.

# BLUEBERRY-WALNUT PANCAKES WITH MAPLE YOGURT

**Recipe by MELISSA LASHER**

**MAKES 2 SERVINGS
(2 PANCAKES EACH)
TOTAL TIME: 15 MINUTES**

*These hearty pancakes will help you recover from your longest training runs. The addition of walnuts and maple yogurt topping, which is rich in protein, gives them extra staying power.*

¼ cup 2% plain Greek yogurt

2 tablespoons maple syrup

1 batch Multigrain Buttermilk Pancake Mix batter (page 23)

¾ cup blueberries

1 tablespoon butter

2 tablespoons chopped walnuts

Heat a large skillet or griddle over medium heat.

In a small bowl, stir together the yogurt and maple syrup. Set aside.

Gently stir the blueberries into the prepared pancake batter.

Add the butter to the hot skillet and swirl to coat the bottom. For each pancake, ladle ⅓ cup batter into the skillet. Cook about 3 minutes, or until bubbles form on the surface and the bottom is golden brown. Flip and cook 1 to 2 minutes longer, until cooked through.

Remove pancakes to 2 plates. Top each with maple yogurt and sprinkle with the walnuts.

NUTRITION PER SERVING: 535 calories, 66 g carbs, 8 g fiber, 17 g protein, 25 g total fat, 6.5 g saturated fat, 692 mg sodium

# QUICK BLUEBERRY SAUCE

Recipe by NATE APPLEMAN

**MAKES ⅔ CUP**
**TOTAL TIME: 5 MINUTES**

- 1 cup blueberries
- 2 teaspoons honey
- 2 teaspoons fresh lemon juice

*Runner's World contributing chef Nate Appleman likes to cook blueberries into a sauce to intensify the fruit's flavor. Drizzle over pancakes, waffles, French toast, yogurt, or even ice cream.*

In a small saucepan, combine the blueberries and honey. Cook over medium heat for about 5 minutes, gently stirring, until the berries break down and become thick and syrupy.

Add the lemon juice and stir to combine. Let the mixture cool, then transfer to a container and store in the refrigerator for up to 1 week. Reheat, if desired, before using.

NUTRITION PER 2½-TABLESPOON SERVING: 32 calories, 8 g carbs, 1 g fiber, 0 g protein, 0 g total fat, 0 g saturated fat, 1 mg sodium

# GOOD MORNING SWEET POTATO

Recipe by MARK BITTMAN

**MAKES 1 SERVING**
**TOTAL TIME: 15 MINUTES**

1 medium sweet potato

¼ cup chopped walnuts

1 tablespoon maple syrup

Pinch of salt

*Sweet potatoes for breakfast? Absolutely. These carb-packed vegetables are loaded with runner-friendly nutrients—and provide a welcome break from typical morning fare. "The flavors in this recipe will remind you of Thanksgiving," says* Runner's World *contributing food writer Mark Bittman.*

Pierce the sweet potato all over with a fork. Microwave on high for 5 to 10 minutes, turning over once or twice, or until the center is soft.

Meanwhile, in a saucepan, combine the walnuts, maple syrup, and salt. Cook over medium-low heat until the nuts are coated and fragrant.

Slice open the top of the potato lengthwise, leaving the bottom intact. Mash the nut mixture on top.

NUTRITION PER SERVING: 355 calories, 44 g carbs, 6 g fiber, 7 g protein, 19 g total fat, 2 g saturated fat, 220 mg sodium

# STRAWBERRY-PISTACHIO PITA PIZZAS

### Recipe by MARK BITTMAN

**MAKES 4 SERVINGS**
**TOTAL TIME: 15 MINUTES**

- 4 large whole wheat pitas (8 inches)
- 2 tablespoons extra-virgin olive oil
- ½ cup warm water
- 2 tablespoons turbinado sugar (optional)
- 2 cups strawberries or other berries, chopped
- ½ cup chopped unsalted pistachios

Runner's World *contributing food writer Mark Bittman refuels after a morning run with this healthy makeover of your favorite toaster pastry. "Inspired by Pop-Tarts, these toasted pita pizzas topped with fresh berry jam are better for you and almost as simple," says Bittman. Strawberries are a rich source of antioxidants that reduce inflammation and repair muscle damage. Taste the fruit—if the berries are very sweet, you don't need to add sugar.*

Preheat the oven to 425°F.

Brush the tops of the pitas with the oil and spread them out on a large baking sheet.

Measure the water into a medium saucepan and whisk in the sugar (if using). Bring to a boil over medium-high heat. Stir in the strawberries and cook for 2 to 3 minutes, mashing and stirring until the fruit softens. Drain well (reserve the liquid for another use, such as smoothies).

Spread the strawberry jam on the pitas and sprinkle with the pistachios. Press the nuts into the jam a bit so they don't burn. Bake the pitas for 5 to 10 minutes, or until the pitas brown around the edges and the nuts turn golden. Cut each pita into quarters and serve warm or at room temperature.

**NUTRITION PER SERVING:** 341 calories, 46 g carbs, 8 g fiber, 10 g protein, 16 g total fat, 2 g saturated fat, 291 mg sodium

# 2

# SMOOTHIES and JUICES

# ISLAND SMOOTHIE

**Recipe by THE RODALE TEST KITCHEN**

**MAKES 1 SERVING**
**TOTAL TIME: 10 MINUTES**

- ½ cup 1% milk
- ½ cup low-fat plain kefir
- 1 teaspoon honey or coconut sugar
- ½ cup frozen or fresh pineapple chunks
- ½ cup frozen mango chunks
- ½ cup unsweetened coconut water (as ice cubes)

*Rich in the electrolyte potassium, coconut water is an ideal addition to smoothies. Freeze coconut water in an ice cube tray and keep a bag of the cubes in your freezer to add to smoothies like this one. The lightly sweet, nutty flavor pairs perfectly with tropical fruits. If you don't have the coconut water ice cubes prepared, just add ½ cup coconut water. The smoothie won't be as thick, but the frozen fruit will still make it refreshingly cold.*

In a blender, combine the milk, kefir, honey, pineapple, mango, and ice cubes. Blend until smooth.

NUTRITION PER SERVING: 259 calories, 51 g carbs, 3 g fiber, 11 g protein, 4 g total fat, 2 g saturated fat, 134 mg sodium

**QUICK TIP** For the best smoothie results, add ingredients to the blender in the order listed. Liquids should go in first, then soft ingredients, like fresh berries, followed by harder or frozen produce and ice last.

# SPRING RUN SMOOTHIE

Recipe by JOANNA SAYAGO GOLUB

**MAKES 1 SERVING**
**TOTAL TIME: 10 MINUTES**

- 1 cup soy milk
- ¼ cup silken tofu
- 1 cup fresh or frozen strawberries, halved
- ½ cup fresh or frozen sliced rhubarb
- ¼ cup baby spinach
- 1 tablespoon chia seeds
- 1 tablespoon fresh lemon juice
- 2 teaspoons agave syrup
- ½ cup ice cubes (optional)

*There's no happier time for runners than that first run after winter's thaw, when hints of spring are in the air. Celebrate it with a smoothie that highlights the early fresh produce of the season, including sweet strawberries, tender baby spinach, and tart rhubarb. Soy milk and tofu provide a vegan protein boost, while chia seeds add healthy fats and fiber. If you use frozen produce in place of fresh, omit the ice.*

In a blender, combine the soy milk, tofu, strawberries, rhubarb, spinach, chia seeds, lemon juice, agave, and ice (if using). Blend until smooth.

NUTRITION PER SERVING: 329 calories, 46 g carbs, 9 g fiber, 18 g protein, 11 g total fat, 1 g saturated fat, 122 mg sodium

# WATERMELON-MINT SLUSHY

Recipe by MATTHEW KADEY, M.S., R.D.

**MAKES 2 SERVINGS**
**TOTAL TIME: 10 MINUTES**

- 2 cups ice cubes
- 1 cup seltzer or flat water
- 1 cup cubed watermelon
- 2 tablespoons chopped fresh mint
- 1 tablespoon agave syrup or honey
- Juice of ½ lemon

*Research shows that drinking an ice-cold beverage, like slushies, before exercising in the heat can make a run in high temperatures more comfortable by preventing overheating. While any fruit slushy will provide carbs needed to energize your run, those made with watermelon offer lycopene to protect your skin from UV damage, as well as anthocyanins to help tame inflammation.*

In a blender, pulse the ice to the size of pebbles. Add the water, watermelon, mint, agave, and lemon juice. Pulse a few times until slushy.

NUTRITION PER SERVING: 58 calories, 15 g carbs, 0 g fiber, 1 g protein, 0 g total fat, 0 g saturated fat, 9 mg sodium

**QUICK TIP** In place of watermelon, use 1 cup pitted tart cherries—they provide antioxidants that can help reduce muscle soreness.

# GREEN TEA SMOOTHIE

Recipe by JOANNA SAYAGO GOLUB

**MAKES 2 SERVINGS**
**TOTAL TIME: 10 MINUTES**

1 cup cold green tea

2 kiwi fruits, peeled and cut into chunks

1½ cups honeydew melon chunks

½ avocado

1 tablespoon agave syrup or honey

1 small banana, frozen

*Green tea is high in an antioxidant compound known as EGCG. Studies show this compound has a range of potential health benefits, including boosting athletic endurance, increasing fat and calorie burning, decreasing risk of cancer, and reducing inflammation.*

In a blender, combine the tea, kiwi, melon, avocado, agave, and banana. Blend until smooth.

NUTRITION PER SERVING: 226 calories, 46 g carbs, 7 g fiber, 3 g protein, 6 g total fat, 1 g saturated fat, 30 mg sodium

# SPICY CARROT COOLER

Recipe by ILANA KATZ, M.S., R.D., C.S.S.D.

**MAKES 1 SERVING**
**TOTAL TIME: 10 MINUTES**

¾ cup carrot juice

¼ cup water

¼ avocado

1 tablespoon fresh lemon juice

1 tablespoon grated fresh ginger

Pinch of cayenne pepper

½ cup ice cubes

*The carrot juice in this savory, low-calorie smoothie is rich in beta-carotene, which your body converts to vitamin A to help regulate the immune system. Fresh ginger adds a sweet, peppery flavor and may help reduce post-exercise muscle pain. Avocado adds a silky texture and heart-healthy monounsaturated fats. Studies show that capsaicin in cayenne pepper briefly boosts metabolism, helping you burn a few extra calories.*

In a blender, combine the carrot juice, water, avocado, lemon juice, ginger, cayenne, and ice. Blend until smooth.

NUTRITION PER SERVING: 118 calories, 16 g carbs, 3 g fiber, 2 g protein, 5 g total fat, 0.5 g saturated fat, 122 mg sodium.

# SUNNY CITRUS SMOOTHIE

**Recipe by THE RODALE TEST KITCHEN**

**MAKES 2 SERVINGS**
**TOTAL TIME: 15 MINUTES**

- 2 oranges
- 1 red grapefruit
- ½ cup unsweetened pomegranate juice
- 1 cup 0% lemon Greek yogurt or other citrus-flavored yogurt
- 1 cup ice cubes

*With its frothy texture and sweet citrus flavor, this bright-tasting smoothie is reminiscent of a classic Orange Julius—but much fresher and with less added sugar.*

Cut the top and bottom off an orange, then stand it on one end. Starting at the top, carefully cut down along the inside of the peel, between the white pith and the fruit. Continue until the entire orange is peeled. Over a bowl or glass measuring cup, cut between the membranes of the orange, releasing the segments into the bowl. Discard any seeds, then, over the bowl, squeeze as much juice as possible from the membranes. Discard. (If any of the peels have fruit on them, squeeze their juice into the bowl, too.) Repeat with the second orange and the grapefruit.

Transfer the citrus segments and juices to a blender. Add the pomegranate juice, yogurt, and ice cubes. Blend until smooth and frothy.

NUTRITION PER SERVING: 235 calories, 49 g carbs, 4 g fiber, 12 g protein, 0 g total fat, 0 g saturated fat, 66 mg sodium

**QUICK TIP** Short on time? Feel free to juice the oranges and grapefruit instead of segmenting them.

# POWER BREAKFAST SMOOTHIE

Recipe by NATE APPLEMAN

**MAKES 2 SERVINGS**
**TOTAL TIME: 10 MINUTES**

1 cup water

¼ cup low-fat plain yogurt

¼ cup fresh blueberries

½ cup quick-cooking oats

2 tablespoons unsweetened shredded coconut

1 tablespoon almond butter

1 tablespoon honey

¼ teaspoon salt

1 small banana, frozen

½ cup frozen mango chunks

*"This is my go-to breakfast,"* says Runner's World *contributing chef Nate Appleman. "It's easy to make and gives me long-lasting energy when I'm training." Quick oats are cut into smaller pieces than old-fashioned rolled oats, so they're easier to blend, but you can use old-fashioned oats if you don't have the quick version on hand.*

In a blender, combine the water, yogurt, blueberries, oats, coconut, almond butter, honey, salt, banana, and mango. Blend until smooth.

NUTRITION PER SERVING: 306 calories, 51 g carbs, 6 g fiber, 7 g protein, 10 g total fat, 4 g saturated fat, 338 mg sodium

# MOCHA MADNESS RECOVERY SHAKE

Recipe by LIZ APPLEGATE, PH.D.

**MAKES 1 SERVING**
**TOTAL TIME: 10 MINUTES**

¼ cup espresso or very strong coffee, cooled

1 cup 2% vanilla Greek yogurt

2 tablespoons sweetened ground chocolate or 1 ounce chocolate, finely chopped

1 banana

½ cup ice cubes

*Research shows that consuming carbohydrates with caffeine increases the rate at which muscle glycogen is restored, helping speed recovery. Add in a good dose of protein from Greek yogurt and this shake has everything you need to recover from a long, hard run.*

In a blender, combine the espresso, yogurt, chocolate, banana, and ice cubes. Blend until smooth.

NUTRITION PER SERVING: 422 calories, 80 g carbs, 4 g fiber, 19 g protein, 5 g total fat, 3 g saturated fat, 159 mg sodium

Cranberry-Beet
Smoothie, page 41

Sunny Citrus
Smoothie, page 36

Green Tea
Smoothie, page 35

Gingered Winter
Greens Smoothie,
page 40

Watermelon-Mint
Slushy, page 34

Spicy Carrot
Cooler, page 35

# APPLE CRISP SMOOTHIE

Recipe by MATTHEW KADEY, M.S., R.D.

**MAKES 2 SERVINGS**
**TOTAL TIME: 10 MINUTES**

- 1 cup apple cider
- ½ cup 2% vanilla Greek yogurt
- ¼ cup old-fashioned rolled oats
- 2 tablespoons chopped pecans
- ¼ teaspoon ground cinnamon
- ⅛ teaspoon ground nutmeg
- 1 cup ice cubes

*Sweet cider, nutty pecans, and rich spices combine to create a smoothie that tastes unmistakably like its namesake fall dessert. The oats give the smoothie staying power and provide beta-glucan, a type of fiber that may improve running endurance. You can even try this smoothie warm: Leave out the ice cubes and heat the cider with 1 cup water. Blend with the other ingredients.*

In a blender, combine the cider, yogurt, oats, pecans, cinnamon, nutmeg, and ice. Blend until smooth.

NUTRITION PER SERVING: 204 calories, 31 g carbs, 2 g fiber, 7 g protein, 6 g total fat, 1 g saturated fat, 45 mg sodium

# GINGERED WINTER GREENS SMOOTHIE

Recipe by MATTHEW KADEY, M.S., R.D.

**MAKES 1 SERVING**
**TOTAL TIME: 10 MINUTES**

- 1 cup unsweetened coconut water
- ½ cup low-fat plain yogurt
- 1 kiwi fruit, peeled
- 1 large kale leaf, center rib removed
- 1 teaspoon minced fresh ginger
- 1 teaspoon honey
- Pinch of salt
- ½ cup ice cubes

*Kale and other cruciferous vegetables contain compounds called glucosinolates that have been shown to have anticancer properties. Adding fresh ginger and a kiwi—which provides more than a day's worth of vitamin C—helps soften the natural bitterness of the leafy green.*

In a blender, combine the coconut water, yogurt, kiwi, kale, ginger, honey, salt, and ice. Blend until smooth.

NUTRITION PER SERVING: 188 calories, 38 g carbs, 3 g fiber, 8 g protein, 2 g total fat, 1 g saturated fat, 272 mg sodium

# CRANBERRY-BEET SMOOTHIE

**Recipe by MATTHEW KADEY, M.S., R.D.**

**MAKES 2 SERVINGS**
**TOTAL TIME: 10 MINUTES**

- ½ cup water
- ½ cup orange or tangerine juice
- 1 small beet, chopped
- ½ cup fresh cranberries
- 1 cup baby spinach
- 2 teaspoons agave syrup or honey
- ½ teaspoon grated fresh ginger
- ½ teaspoon ground allspice
- 1 cup ice cubes

*This low-calorie prerun combo will charge up your workout without weighing you down. Beets and spinach are an impressive duo—they contain nitrates that boost oxygen delivery and improve muscle functioning and strength. Cranberries supply fast-digesting carbs and potent antioxidants that have heart-health benefits.*

In a blender, combine the water, orange juice, beet, cranberries, spinach, agave, ginger, allspice, and ice. Blend until smooth.

NUTRITION DATA PER SERVING: 81 calories, 20 g carbs, 3 g fiber, 1 g protein, 0 g total fat, 0 g saturated fat, 51 mg sodium

# SWEET POTATO PIE SMOOTHIE

### Recipe by MATTHEW KADEY, M.S., R.D.

**MAKES 1 SERVING**
**TOTAL TIME: 10 MINUTES**

- 1 cup sweetened coconut milk beverage (from a carton, not canned)
- ½ cup cooked peeled sweet potato, cooled
- 1 tablespoon chopped walnuts or pecans
- ½ teaspoon vanilla extract
- ¼ teaspoon ground cinnamon
- ⅛ teaspoon ground nutmeg
- ½ banana, frozen

*No time for a sit-down lunch? Try this smoothie. It provides all the components of a well-rounded meal—carbs, fiber, protein, and healthy fats. Just blend it up and pour into a thermos to go. Don't use canned coconut milk—it's too rich for this recipe. Instead, look for coconut milk packaged in cartons sold near other dairy milk alternatives.*

In a blender, combine the coconut milk, sweet potato, nuts, vanilla, cinnamon, nutmeg, and banana. Blend until smooth.

NUTRITION PER SERVING: 262 calories, 44 g carbs, 7 g fiber, 4 g protein, 9 g total fat, 4.5 g saturated fat, 37 mg sodium

**QUICK TIP** Sweet potato, pumpkin, and butternut squash can infuse smoothies with sweet, fall flavor. Peel and steam up a bunch, then mash and freeze in muffin cups so you can add some to smoothies whenever you like.

# AUNTIE OXIE JUICE

Recipe by JOE CROSS, AUTHOR OF *101 JUICE RECIPES*

**MAKES 2 SERVINGS**
**TOTAL TIME: 5 MINUTES**

- 2 cups red grapes
- 2 cups blueberries
- 2 cups pomegranate seeds
- 4 stalks celery

*Vibrantly colored with a pop of refreshing flavor, this juice offers a wealth of antioxidants and nutritional benefits that are ideal for replenishing your body after a run. The antioxidant fruits aid in combating pain in your joints and muscles.*

In a juicer, process the grapes, blueberries, pomegranate seeds, and celery. Drink immediately.

NUTRITION PER SERVING: 189 calories, 30 g net carbs, 0 g fiber, 2 g protein, 1 g total fat, 0 g saturated fat, 51 mg sodium

**QUICK TIP** Soft fruits, such as berries, and leafy greens can be difficult to juice. After putting them through the juicer, add a fruit or vegetable that will produce a higher juice yield (such as apples, citrus, celery, or cucumber), which will help push the berry and green juices through the receptacle.

# SPORTY SPICE JUICE

Recipe by JOE CROSS, AUTHOR OF
*THE REBOOT WITH JOE JUICE DIET COOKBOOK*

**MAKES 2 SERVINGS**
**TOTAL TIME: 10 MINUTES**

3 stalks celery

2 beets

1 carrot

1 handful fresh basil

1 lemon, peeled

1 orange, peeled

*Loaded with electrolytes, including sodium, potassium, and magnesium, this juice is an excellent choice for postrun rehydration. Celery contains compounds that may promote bone health, while citrus fruits are rich in vitamin C, a nutrient that plays a key role in forming collagen needed to keep joints working properly. Basil aids digestion and has antibacterial and anti-inflammatory properties.*

In a juicer, process the celery, beets, carrot, basil, lemon, and orange. Drink immediately.

NUTRITION PER SERVING: 99 calories, 19 g net carbs, 3 g fiber, 3 g protein, 1 g total fat, 0 g saturated fat, 134 mg sodium

# JUST BEET IT JUICE

Recipe by JOE CROSS, AUTHOR OF
*THE REBOOT WITH JOE JUICE DIET COOKBOOK*

**MAKES 2 SERVINGS**
**TOTAL TIME: 10 MINUTES**

2 beets

2 pears, stemmed

1 knob ginger

1 cucumber

*Beets contain nitric-oxide compounds that help oxygenate blood and may enhance exercise performance, while ginger has anti-inflammatory properties and may calm an upset stomach.*

In a juicer, process the beets, pears, ginger, and cucumber. Drink immediately.

NUTRITION PER SERVING: 154 calories, 31 g net carbs, 2 g fiber, 4 g protein, 1 g total fat, 0 g saturated fat, 66 mg sodium

# TOMATO-BASIL JUICE

Recipe by CHERIE CALBOM, M.S., C.N., AUTHOR OF
*THE JUICE LADY'S BIG BOOK OF JUICES AND GREEN SMOOTHIES*

**MAKES 2 SERVINGS**
**TOTAL TIME: 5 MINUTES**

2 tomatoes

1 cup spinach

4 sprigs basil

1 lemon or lime, peeled

*Tomatoes are a good source of the antioxidant vitamin C. This nutrient helps boost the absorption of iron (needed to maintain exercise endurance) found in leafy greens such as spinach.*

In a juicer, process the tomatoes, spinach, basil, and lemon. Drink immediately.

NUTRITION PER SERVING: 34 calories, 6 g net carbs, 0 g fiber, 2 g protein, ½ g total fat, 0 g saturated fat, 19 mg sodium

# GREAT GREENS JUICE

Recipe by JOE CROSS, AUTHOR OF *101 JUICE RECIPES*

**MAKES 2 SERVINGS**
**TOTAL TIME: 10 MINUTES**

2 stalks celery

6 Swiss chard leaves

½ fennel bulb

2 cups spinach

1 cucumber

1 bunch fresh basil

1 green apple, cored

*Consume this powerhouse of phytonutrients before a workout for a boost of energy. The combination of green vegetables can help fight inflammation to ward off any post-workout pain.*

In a juicer, process the celery, Swiss chard, fennel, spinach, cucumber, basil, and apple. Drink immediately.

NUTRITION PER SERVING: 102 calories, 16 g net carbs, 0 g fiber, 6 g protein, 1 g total fat, 0 g saturated fat, 394 mg sodium

Great Greens
Juice, page 45

Cucumber-
Coconut Juice,
opposite page

Watermelon-
Cherry Juice,
opposite page

# WATERMELON-CHERRY JUICE

Recipe by LESLIE BONCI, M.P.H., R.D., C.S.S.D., L.D.N.

**MAKES 2 SERVINGS**
**TOTAL TIME: 5 MINUTES**

2 cups watermelon cubes

1 cup pitted tart cherries

1 orange, peeled

*Tart cherries contain anthocyanins, while watermelon provides the amino acid L-citrulline—both nutrients may help reduce postrun muscle soreness. Oranges are rich in vitamin C, which plays a role in collagen formation and helps protect your immune system.*

In a juicer, process the watermelon, cherries, and orange. Drink immediately.

NUTRITION PER SERVING: 124 calories, 29 g net carbs, 1 g fiber, 3 g protein, 1 g total fat, 0 g saturated fat, 11 mg sodium

# CUCUMBER-COCONUT JUICE

Recipe by LESLIE BONCI, M.P.H., R.D., C.S.S.D., L.D.N.

**MAKES 2 SERVINGS**
**TOTAL TIME: 10 MINUTES**

1 green apple, cored

2 fresh mint leaves

½ cup honeydew melon chunks

½ cucumber

1 cup unsweetened coconut water

Dash of turmeric

*Water-rich cucumber helps you rehydrate, while coconut water adds the electrolyte potassium. Finishing with a dash of turmeric can help curb inflammation.*

In a juicer, process the apple, mint, honeydew, and cucumber. Pour into a glass and stir in the coconut water. Sprinkle with the turmeric. Drink immediately.

NUTRITION PER SERVING: 76 calories, 19 g net carbs, 0 g fiber, 1 g protein, 0 g total fat, 0 g saturated fat, 23 mg sodium

# 3

# SNACKS and SWEETS

### *Energy Bars and Balls*

### *Spreads and Dips*

### *Sweet and Savory Snacks*

# HONEY ENERGY BARS

Recipe by LIZ APPLEGATE, PH.D.

**MAKES 9 SQUARES**
**TOTAL TIME: 30 MINUTES**

- 2 large eggs
- 3 tablespoons honey
- 2 tablespoons canola oil
- 2 teaspoons grated orange zest
- 2 cups granola, such as Almond-Cherry Granola (page 2)
- ⅔ cup roughly chopped walnuts

*These sweet, crunchy, and slightly chewy bars are the perfect prerun pick-me-up. Honey provides simple sugars (fructose and glucose) that are quickly absorbed and will energize your workout. Honey also contains oligosaccharides, a type of sugar that may promote the growth of healthy bacteria in the intestinal tract. Studies show that these carbohydrates serve as fuel for immune-boosting bacteria in the gut.*

Preheat the oven to 375°F. Coat an 8-inch square baking pan with cooking spray.

In a bowl, lightly whisk the eggs. Whisk in the honey, oil, and zest. Stir in the granola and walnuts. Mix until thoroughly combined.

Spread the mixture in the baking pan and bake for 15 minutes, or until golden brown and set. Cool for 10 minutes before cutting into 9 squares. Store tightly covered in the refrigerator.

NUTRITION PER BAR: 193 calories, 23 g carbs, 2 g fiber, 5 g protein, 10 g total fat, 1 g saturated fat, 18 mg sodium

# PACKFIT BARS

Recipe by WILL ARTLEY

**MAKES 16 SQUARES**
**TOTAL TIME: 25 MINUTES**

- ¼ cup golden flaxseeds
- ¼ cup brown flaxseeds
- ¼ cup chia seeds
- ½ cup steel-cut oats
- 1 cup chopped cashews
- ¼ cup sunflower seeds
- ¼ cup dried tart cherries or roughly chopped dried apricots
- 26 pitted dates or fresh figs, roughly chopped
- ⅛ teaspoon ground cinnamon
- ½ cup unsweetened flaked coconut (optional)
- ¼ cup vanilla raw protein powder
- ¼ cup unsweetened cocoa powder
- ¼ cup honey
- Pinch of salt

*When Will Artley, executive chef at BLT Steak in Washington, D.C., took up running and triathlons to lose weight a few years ago, he searched for the right fuel to energize him during workouts. Dissatisfied with store-bought options, he created his own energy bar packed with honey, dates, and cherries. Artley, who races with Tri360 in Arlington, Virginia, named the bars after his wife's health business. "She's been my biggest supporter in my quest to become healthy," says Artley. Now more than 100 pounds lighter, he's on his way to becoming an Ironman and ultrarunner with the help of his coaching program, Speed Sherpa. "For a while, food was killing me," says Artley, "but now I'm harnessing it to make a positive change."*

Line an 8-inch square baking pan with plastic wrap. Coat the inside with cooking spray.

In a food processor, combine the golden and brown flaxseeds, chia seeds, oats, cashews, sunflower seeds, cherries, dates, cinnamon, coconut (if using), protein powder, cocoa powder, honey, and salt. Process for about 1 minute, or until the nuts and fruit are broken into small pieces and the mixture starts to move around the blade in one mass.

Scrape the mixture into the pan and press vigorously to compact. Cover and refrigerate for 15 minutes before cutting into 16 bars. Leave refrigerated until ready to eat.

NUTRITION PER BAR: 237 calories, 44 g carbs, 7 g fiber, 5 g protein, 7 g total fat, 1 g saturated fat, 12 mg sodium

# EL GUAPO'S GREAT ENERGY BARS

Recipe by BILL LYNCH

**MAKES 16 SQUARES**
**TOTAL TIME: 30 MINUTES,**
**PLUS COOLING TIME**

   2 very ripe bananas

   ¾ cup packed dark brown
     sugar

   ½ cup canola oil or melted
     coconut oil

   ½ teaspoon vanilla extract

   ½ teaspoon baking powder

   ½ teaspoon baking soda

   ½ teaspoon salt

   ½ teaspoon ground cinnamon

   ½ teaspoon ground nutmeg

   ¾ cup soy flour or
     all-purpose flour

   1½ cups old-fashioned
     rolled oats

   ½ cup unsweetened flaked
     coconut, toasted, or an
     additional ½ cup oats

   ¾ cup pecans, chopped

   ¾ cup golden raisins

*"Running gives me time to think," says Bill Lynch, chef at Varanese in Louisville, Kentucky, "so I can be more creative in the kitchen." Lynch (whose nickname is El Guapo) started running to lose weight a few years ago and has shed 40 pounds. He was inspired on a long run to create these vegan, gluten-free banana bars. He makes them with soy flour because it's high in protein. "They've got fiber to keep you full, long-lasting energy from the oats, and bananas for quick energy."*

Preheat the oven to 350°F. Coat a 9-inch square baking pan with cooking spray.

In a large bowl, mash the bananas with a fork. Add the brown sugar, oil, and vanilla. With an electric mixer or whisk, combine until smooth.

In a separate large bowl, whisk together the baking powder, baking soda, salt, cinnamon, nutmeg, flour, oats, and coconut (or additional ½ cup oats). Add the banana mixture and stir until just combined. Fold in the pecans and raisins.

Pour the mixture into the baking pan and spread evenly. Bake for 20 minutes, or until the top puffs and turns golden brown. Transfer to a wire rack to cool completely. Cut into 16 squares and wrap individually in plastic wrap to keep fresh.

NUTRITION PER BAR: 231 calories, 26 g carbs, 3 g fiber, 4 g protein, 14 g total fat, 2.5 g saturated fat, 129 mg sodium

# CHOCOLATE CHIP TRAIL MIX BALLS

Recipe by JOANNA SAYAGO GOLUB

**MAKES 24 BALLS**
**TOTAL TIME: 15 MINUTES, PLUS**
**OPTIONAL CHILLING TIME**

½ cup almond butter

⅓ cup agave syrup or honey

1½ cups old-fashioned
   rolled oats

¼ cup pumpkin seeds

¼ cup dark chocolate mini
   chips

¼ cup chopped dried tart
   cherries

¼ cup sliced almonds

½ cup toasted wheat germ

*Salty and sweet, these tasty little snacks pack the essential components of trail mix—nuts, dried fruit, and, yes, chocolate—into an easily portable package. Not only are they a delicious prerun snack, but they also make for a quick breakfast on the go.*

In a bowl, with an electric mixer on low speed, mix together the almond butter and agave syrup for 2 minutes, or until smooth and well combined.

With the mixer still on low, gradually add the oats until well combined, followed by the pumpkin seeds. Add the chocolate chips, cherries, and almonds. Mix for about 1 minute on low, or until just combined.

Line a baking sheet with wax paper. For each ball, use a tablespoon to take a heaping scoop of the mixture and, with your hands, gently roll into a ball. Roll in the wheat germ and set on the baking sheet lined with wax paper.

You can eat the trail mix balls immediately, or transfer any uneaten ones (still on the baking sheet) to the refrigerator for 2 hours, or until set. Transfer the chilled balls to a plastic freezer bag and store in the fridge for up to 2 weeks.

NUTRITION PER SERVING (2 balls): 210 calories, 24 g carbs, 5 g fiber, 7 g protein, 11 g total fat, 2 g saturated fat, 30 mg sodium

# DATE BALLS

**Recipe by AMY FRITCH**

**MAKES 10 BALLS**
**TOTAL TIME: 15 MINUTES**

- ½ cup chopped dates
- 2 tablespoons sunflower seeds
- 2 tablespoons chopped macadamia nuts
- 2 tablespoons chopped cashews
- 1 tablespoon ground flaxseeds (flax meal)
- 2 tablespoons cacao nibs
- 1 teaspoon unsweetened cocoa powder
- 1 teaspoon melted coconut oil
- ½ teaspoon vanilla extract
- 2 tablespoons maple syrup
- ⅓ cup unsweetened shredded coconut

*Unlike many über-sweet energy bars, these snack-size balls will power you through your run without making you feel like you just ate a candy bar. Dates provide just the right amount of natural sweetness (along with anti-oxidants), balanced by hints of cocoa.*

In a food processor, combine the dates, sunflower seeds, macadamia nuts, cashews, flax meal, cacao nibs, cocoa powder, coconut oil, vanilla, and maple syrup. Process for 30 seconds, then stop to scrape down the sides of the bowl. Process for 30 seconds to 1 minute more, or until the ingredients form a ball.

Using your hands, roll the mixture into 10 balls, about 1 tablespoon each. Roll the balls in the coconut. Serve immediately, or store in an airtight container for up to 1 week.

NUTRITION PER SERVING (2 balls): 204 calories, 21 g carbs, 5 g fiber, 3 g protein, 13 g total fat, 6 g saturated fat, 10 mg sodium

QUICK TIP You can make these with any kind of nut (almonds, walnuts, pecans), as well as toss in a nutrient boost, such as chia seeds, goji berries, or dried cherries—whatever you have on hand.

# LIZ'S FAMOUS GUACAMOLE

Recipe by LIZ APPLEGATE, PH.D.

**MAKES ABOUT 2 CUPS**
**TOTAL TIME: 10 MINUTES**

2 avocados

½ cup diced red onion

1 large tomato, chopped

1 clove garlic, minced

Juice of 1 lime

½ teaspoon toasted sesame oil

3 tablespoons chopped fresh cilantro

¼ teaspoon salt

¼ teaspoon ground black pepper

*Loaded with inflammation-fighting antioxidants and heart-healthy fats, this guac is sure to please your runner friends at your next postrace cookout. Cut the avocado into quarters; gently pull back the peel being careful to retain all the deep green flesh, which has the richest concentration of carotenoid antioxidants.*

In a bowl, mash the avocados with a fork, leaving it slightly chunky. Stir in the onion, tomato, garlic, lime juice, sesame oil, cilantro, salt, and pepper.

NUTRITION PER ⅓-CUP SERVING: 124 calories, 9 g carbs, 5 g fiber, 2 g protein, 10 g total fat, 1.5 g saturated fat, 104 mg sodium

**QUICK TIP** Use guacamole as a dip with fresh veggies or multi-grain chips, or spread it on sandwiches, burgers, or grilled fish, chicken, or meat.

# TAHINI AND SUN-DRIED TOMATO DIP

Recipe by NATE APPLEMAN

**MAKES ABOUT 1 CUP**
**TOTAL TIME: 10 MINUTES**

- ½ cup oil-packed sun-dried tomatoes
- ½ cup tahini
- 1 clove garlic
- 2 tablespoons fresh lemon juice
- ⅛ teaspoon salt

*Sun-dried tomatoes are a concentrated source of nutrients, providing vitamins C and K, iron, and lycopene, an antioxidant associated with lower risk of certain cancers. You'll find them available dry or packed in oil (the latter work best in this recipe, since they are softer and easier to blend). Serve this dip with vegetables or on whole grain crackers. The recipe can double as a salad dressing: simply add water, a little at a time, to thin to desired consistency.*

In a food processor, combine the sun-dried tomatoes, tahini, garlic, and lemon juice. Process until blended. Season with the salt and stir to combine.

NUTRITION PER 2-TABLESPOON SERVING: 139 calories, 5 g carbs, 1 g fiber, 3 g protein, 13 g total fat, 2 g saturated fat, 54 mg sodium

# EDAMAME-BASIL DIP

Recipe by THE RODALE TEST KITCHEN

**MAKES 1 CUP**
**TOTAL TIME: 15 MINUTES**

- 1 cup frozen shelled edamame
- ⅔ cup packed fresh basil leaves
- ¼ cup extra-virgin olive oil
- 3 tablespoons fresh lemon juice
- ¼ teaspoon salt

*Keep a few bags of edamame in your freezer and you can make this simple dip anytime. Basil and lemon juice add fresh, bright flavor. Serve it as a party appetizer, or keep it on hand for a healthy snack while cooking dinner during the week.*

Bring a small pot of water to a boil over high heat. Add the edamame and cook for 4 minutes, or until tender. Drain and rinse with cold water to cool.

Transfer the edamame to a food processor along with the basil, oil, lemon juice, and salt. Puree until smooth.

NUTRITION PER 2-TABLESPOON SERVING: 87 calories, 3 g carbs, 1 g fiber, 2 g protein, 8 g total fat, 1 g saturated fat, 81 mg sodium

Edamame-Basil Dip,
opposite page

Tahini and Sun-
Dried Tomato Dip,
opposite page

Lemon-Carrot
Hummus, page 60

# LEMON-CARROT HUMMUS

## Recipe by THE RODALE TEST KITCHEN

**MAKES 1¾ CUPS**
**TOTAL TIME: 20 MINUTES**

- 1 carrot, thinly sliced
- 3 cloves garlic, smashed and peeled
- 1 can (15 ounces) chickpeas, drained and rinsed
- 1 tablespoon toasted sesame oil
- 3 tablespoons fresh lemon juice
- 3 tablespoons low-fat plain yogurt
- ¼ teaspoon salt

*Carrot adds a subtle sweetness (and orange hue) to this lighter rendition of the classic chickpea dip. Look for toasted sesame oil, sometimes called dark sesame oil, in the Asian section of most supermarkets. Use the hummus as a spread on wraps and sandwiches. Or dip in pita bread and pretzels for a prerun snack.*

In a small saucepan, combine the carrot and garlic with water to cover. Simmer over medium heat for 10 minutes, or until tender.

Reserving the cooking liquid, drain and transfer the vegetables to a food processor. Add the chickpeas, sesame oil, lemon juice, yogurt, and salt. Process until smooth, adding up to 2 tablespoons of the reserved liquid if necessary

NUTRITION PER 2-TABLESPOON SERVING: 56 calories, 8 g carbs, 2 g fiber, 2 g protein, 2 g total fat, 0 g saturated fat, 56 mg sodium

# CHOCOLATE AVOCADO SPREAD

Recipe by LIZ APPLEGATE, PH.D.

**MAKES 2 CUPS**
**TOTAL TIME: 10 MINUTES**

- 2 avocados
- ½ cup unsweetened cocoa powder
- ½ cup honey
- 1 teaspoon vanilla extract

*When you must have chocolate, this antioxidant-packed treat will more than satisfy. Avocados lend the dip a smooth and silky texture, but thanks to the cocoa powder and honey, all you taste is chocolaty goodness. Use it as a dip for fresh strawberries or spread on your favorite muffin, scone, or quick bread.*

Halve and pit the avocados. Over a food processor, squeeze the halves so the flesh drops into the bowl. Add the cocoa powder, honey, and vanilla. Process for about 1 minute, stopping to scrape down the sides of the bowl as needed, or until smooth. Use immediately or store in the fridge for up to 1 week.

NUTRITION PER 2-TABLESPOON SERVING: 67 calories, 12 g carbs, 2 g fiber, 1 g protein, 3 g total fat, 0.5 g saturated fat, 2 mg sodium

# MAPLE-CINNAMON WALNUT BUTTER

**Recipe by JESSICA MIGALA**

**MAKES ½ CUP**
**TOTAL TIME: 5 MINUTES**

1 cup roasted walnuts

1 teaspoon maple syrup

½ teaspoon ground cinnamon

Pinch of salt

*You can turn any nut—almonds, pistachios, walnuts—into a creamy spread loaded with heart-healthy fats and key vitamins and minerals. Walnuts are one of the few vegetarian sources of omega-3s, fats that help calm postexercise inflammation. Be sure to use roasted walnuts—raw ones can impart a bitter flavor. Pair with whole grain raisin bread or stir into oatmeal.*

In a food processor, blend the walnuts for 3 to 5 minutes, stopping to scrape the bowl as needed.

Add the maple syrup, cinnamon, and salt. Process about 2 minutes longer, or until smooth.

NUTRITION PER 2-TABLESPOON SERVING: 200 calories, 5 g carbs, 2 g fiber, 4 g protein, 19 g total fat, 2 g saturated fat, 35 mg sodium

# SMOKY SRIRACHA PEANUT BUTTER

**Recipe by JESSICA MIGALA**

**MAKES ½ CUP**
**TOTAL TIME: 5 MINUTES**

1 cup unsalted dry-roasted peanuts

½ tablespoon extra-virgin olive oil

1 tablespoon Sriracha sauce

¼ teaspoon smoked paprika

Pinch of salt

*This savory peanut butter gets its intense flavor from smoked paprika, while Sriracha adds just the right amount of spice. It's delicious on celery eaten as a snack, spread on top of a burger, or added to chicken stir-fry. Because of their fiber, protein, and fat content, peanuts are especially satiating; research shows that people who eat peanuts regularly have a lower body mass index.*

In a food processor, blend the peanuts for 3 to 5 minutes, stopping to scrape the bowl as needed.

Add the oil and process for 1 minute. Add the Sriracha, smoked paprika, and salt and process 1 to 2 minutes longer, or until smooth.

NUTRITION PER 2-TABLESPOON SERVING: 230 calories, 9 g carbs, 3 g fiber, 9 g protein, 20 g total fat, 3 g saturated fat, 115 mg sodium

Almond-Coconut
Butter, page 64

Smoky Sriracha
Peanut Butter,
opposite page

Sweet and Salty
Pistachio Butter,
page 64

Maple-Cinnamon
Walnut Butter,
opposite page

# ALMOND-COCONUT BUTTER

Recipe by JESSICA MIGALA

**MAKES 1 CUP**
**TOTAL TIME: 10 MINUTES**

- 1 cup unsalted roasted almonds
- 1 cup unsweetened shredded coconut
- ½ tablespoon coconut oil, melted
- 1 teaspoon honey
- ½ teaspoon vanilla extract
- ¼ teaspoon ground cinnamon

*Almonds are a rich source of vitamin E, which assists with red blood cell formation and helps widen blood vessels to improve heart health. Coconut oil will cause this butter to harden in the fridge. When ready to use, microwave a tablespoon or two on high for about 20 seconds to soften. Pair with whole grain graham crackers or pumpkin bread.*

In a food processor, blend the almonds for 3 to 5 minutes, or until smooth, stopping to scrape the bowl as needed. Transfer the almond butter to a bowl. (Don't wash the processor bowl.)

Add the shredded coconut to the processor and blend for 5 minutes. Add the coconut oil and process 1 minute longer (the mixture should have a near-liquid consistency).

Return the almond butter to the processor along with the honey, vanilla, and cinnamon. Blend briefly until combined.

NUTRITION PER 2-TABLESPOON SERVING: 190 calories, 7 g carbs, 3 g fiber, 4 g protein, 17 g total fat, 8 g saturated fat, 0 mg sodium

# SWEET AND SALTY PISTACHIO BUTTER

Recipe by JESSICA MIGALA

**MAKES ½ CUP**
**TOTAL TIME: 5 MINUTES**

- 1 cup salted roasted pistachios
- 2 tablespoons canola oil
- 1 tablespoon honey

*Pistachios are a good source of copper, a trace mineral that keeps your immune system in tip-top shape. The nut is also high in thiamin, a B vitamin that assists your body in converting carbs into running fuel. Pair this spread with goat cheese, pretzels, or multigrain crackers.*

In a food processor, blend the pistachios and oil for 4 minutes, stopping to scrape down the bowl as needed. Scrape the butter into a bowl and stir in the honey.

NUTRITION PER 2-TABLESPOON SERVING: 250 calories, 13 g carbs, 3 g fiber, 6 g protein, 21 g total fat, 2 g saturated fat, 130 mg sodium

# SUPER "CHEESY" KALE CHIPS

Recipe by JENNIFER KUSHNIER

**MAKES 2 SERVINGS**
**TOTAL TIME: 25 MINUTES**

- ½ bunch kale (about ½ pound)
- 1 tablespoon extra-virgin olive oil
- 1 to 2 tablespoons nutritional yeast
- ½ teaspoon salt

*Crunchy kale chips get a big flavor boost thanks to a sprinkling of nutritional yeast, which adds a range of B vitamins and protein and tastes similar to Parmesan cheese. Start with 1 tablespoon of the yeast flakes, then taste, and add up to another tablespoon, if desired. Kale chips are best when fresh out of the oven. You can store any leftovers in an airtight container, but they won't remain as crunchy.*

Preheat the oven to 325°F.

Rinse the kale and rip the center stalks from the leaves. Tear the leaves into similar-size pieces so they will crisp evenly. Place them in a large bowl. (If the leaves are quite wet, gently squeeze them with a paper towel to remove excess moisture.)

Sprinkle with the oil, nutritional yeast, and salt and use tongs to toss the leaves until they are uniformly coated.

Scatter the kale around a baking sheet. Bake, tossing once, for about 20 minutes, or until desired crispness. Remove from the oven and allow to cool on the baking sheet for a minute before serving.

NUTRITION PER SERVING: 119 calories, 9 g carbs, 3 g fiber, 8 g protein, 8 g total fat, 1 g saturated fat, 509 mg sodium

# GARLIC-ROSEMARY PITA CHIPS

Recipe by JOANNA SAYAGO GOLUB

**MAKES 4 SERVINGS**
**TOTAL TIME: 20 MINUTES**

- 4 whole wheat pitas (6 inches)
- 2 tablespoons extra-virgin olive oil
- ½ teaspoon garlic powder
- ½ teaspoon dried rosemary
- ½ teaspoon salt
- ¼ teaspoon ground black pepper

*These pita chips are supersimple to make and taste much fresher than any chip from a bag. Rich in whole grain carbs, they make a great prerun snack. Try them paired with Tahini and Sun-Dried Tomato Dip (page 58).*

Preheat the oven to 350°F.

Brush the tops of the pitas with the oil. In a small bowl, combine the garlic powder, rosemary, salt, and pepper. Sprinkle each pita with the mixture. Cut each pita into 8 wedges and transfer to 2 baking sheets.

Bake for 10 to 12 minutes, or until the wedges are crisp and lightly browned. Let them cool for a few minutes before eating. Store any leftover chips in an airtight container for up to 3 days.

NUTRITION PER SERVING: 236 calories, 36 g carbs, 5 g fiber, 6 g protein, 9 g total fat, 1 g saturated fat, 575 mg sodium

# SESAME-ALMOND MIX

**Recipe by THE RODALE TEST KITCHEN**

**MAKES 5 CUPS**
**TOTAL TIME: 20 MINUTES,**
**PLUS COOLING TIME**

1 large egg white

¼ cup soy sauce

2 teaspoons toasted
sesame oil

4 cups raw almonds

1 cup sunflower seeds

¼ cup sesame seeds

*Next time hunger strikes between meals, reach for a handful of this nut and seed mix. It's high in fiber, protein, and healthy fats—all of which will help tame your appetite and steady your blood sugar to keep cravings under control. Use raw almonds—these are unblanched almonds that still have their dark brown skins (which add flavor and nutrients)—and choose nuts and seeds that have not been toasted.*

Preheat the oven to 350°F.

In a large bowl, whisk the egg white until frothy. Add the soy sauce and sesame oil and whisk until well combined. Add the almonds, sunflower seeds, and sesame seeds, and toss until coated.

Spread the mixture out on an unlined rimmed baking sheet and bake for 15 minutes, stirring once or twice, until golden. They will crisp up as they cool. Cool completely before storing in an airtight container.

NUTRITION PER ⅓-CUP SERVING: 278 calories, 10 g carbs, 5 g fiber, 10 g protein, 24 g total fat, 2 g saturated fat, 225 mg sodium

QUICK TIP Feel free to swap in any nuts or seeds you have on hand.

# CURRY CHIPOTLE POPCORN

Recipe by RACHEL MELTZER WARREN, M.S., R.D.

**MAKES 1 SERVING**
**TOTAL TIME: 5 MINUTES**

- 2 tablespoons plain popcorn kernels
- 1½ teaspoons canola oil
- ½ teaspoon curry powder
- ¼ teaspoon chipotle powder or chili powder
- ⅛ teaspoon salt

*Low in calories and high in fiber, popcorn is the perfect snack for runners trying to lose weight. The key is to stick with plain popcorn and lightly season it yourself to keep it healthy. Adding a sprinkle of ground chipotle is a smart idea if you are watching your weight: Research shows that the compound that gives chile peppers their spicy kick also helps reduce your appetite.*

Place the popcorn kernels in a paper bag. Fold down the top a few times, leaving room in the bag for the kernels to pop. Microwave on high for 2 to 3 minutes, until the popping slows down to a couple seconds between pops. Give the bag a few shakes to encourage unpopped kernels to pop. Be careful not to burn yourself with steam when opening the bag. Transfer the popcorn to a large bowl.

Meanwhile, in a small skillet, combine the oil, curry powder, chipotle powder, and salt. Whisk gently over low heat for 1 to 2 minutes, or until the oil begins to bubble.

Drizzle the spiced oil onto the popcorn. Toss well to coat evenly.

NUTRITION PER SERVING: 160 calories, 20 g carbs, 4 g fiber, 3 g protein, 8 g total fat, 0.5 g saturated fat, 300 mg sodium

# INSTANT FROZEN YOGURT

Recipe by JENNIFER KUSHNIER

**MAKES 4 SERVINGS**
**TOTAL TIME: 5 MINUTES**

- 1½ cups frozen unsweetened strawberries
- 1 cup 2% strawberry-banana Greek yogurt
- 1 tablespoon sugar
- ½ teaspoon vanilla extract (optional)

*Made with Greek yogurt, this guilt-free dessert provides a good dose of protein. Try it with any frozen fruit and flavor of yogurt you have on hand.*

In a food processor, process the strawberries for about 15 seconds, or until broken up into little bits. Scrape down the sides of the bowl.

Add the yogurt, sugar, and vanilla (if using) and process about 15 seconds longer, until blended, thick, and smooth—but not pureed and runny. For a softer serve, eat immediately, or store in the freezer in an airtight container for up to 1 week. Let it stand at room temperature for a few minutes to soften before serving.

Nutrition serving: 112 calories, 18 g carbs, 2 g fiber, 7 g protein, 2 g total fat, 1 g saturated fat, 34 mg sodium

# HIGH-PROTEIN CHOCOLATE PUDDING

Recipe by CLAUDIA WILSON, M.S., R.D., C.S.S.D., C.S.C.S.

**MAKES 6 SERVINGS**
**TOTAL TIME: 5 MINUTES**

- 1 cup plain soy milk
- 1 package (14 to 16 ounces) silken tofu
- ½ cup sugar
- ½ cup unsweetened cocoa powder
- 1 teaspoon vanilla extract
- ¼ teaspoon salt
- Ground cinnamon (optional)

*Why bother with instant pudding when you can make your own creamy, chocolaty version at home in the same amount of time? An added bonus: It's higher in protein, thanks to the addition of tofu. Using soy milk also keeps it dairy-free.*

In a food processor or blender, combine the soy milk, tofu, sugar, cocoa, vanilla, and salt. Blend for 1 minute, scrape down sides, and blend 1 minute more, or until smooth.

Scoop into small serving bowls. Top with a sprinkle of cinnamon, if desired.

NUTRITION PER SERVING: 136 calories, 25 g carbs, 3 g fiber, 6 g protein, 3 g total fat, 1 g saturated fat, 121 mg sodium

# FIGS WITH MASCARPONE AND HONEY

Recipe by THE RODALE TEST KITCHEN

**MAKES 6 SERVINGS**
**TOTAL TIME: 10 MINUTES**

- 12 large fresh figs, cut into quarters
- 6 ounces mascarpone cheese, at room temperature
- 3 tablespoons honey

*Next time you want to treat yourself, try this simple, yet perfectly paired combination. If you can't find figs, fresh in-season strawberries are equally delicious. Any light-colored honey will work, but try a variety such as wild-flower for additional flavor.*

Divide the figs among 6 bowls. Add 1 ounce of mascarpone to each. Drizzle each serving with ½ tablespoon honey.

**Variation** Substitute 12 large strawberries, quartered, for the figs.

NUTRITION PER SERVING: 248 calories, 33 g carbs, 4 g fiber, 3 g protein, 14 g total fat, 7 g saturated fat, 17 mg sodium

# WARM GINGERBREAD PUDDING

Recipe by MATTHEW KADEY, M.S., R.D.

**MAKES 6 SERVINGS**
**TOTAL TIME: 25 MINUTES**

- 2 cups water
- ½ cup teff grain (not flour)
- ⅓ cup canned light coconut milk
- 1 banana
- 3 tablespoons maple syrup
- 3 tablespoons unsweetened cocoa powder
- 2 teaspoons vanilla extract
- ¼ teaspoon ground ginger
- ⅛ teaspoon ground cloves
  Pinch of salt
- ¼ cup chopped hazelnuts
- ¼ cup crystallized ginger, chopped

*The secret ingredient in the chocolaty pudding? Teff, a whole grain, gluten-free staple among Ethiopian runners. Teff has more energy-boosting iron than other whole grains, and it releases starches as it cooks, creating a thick pudding consistency. If you prefer chilled pudding, do not warm up the coconut milk and cool the blended pudding in the refrigerator for 2 hours before serving.*

In a saucepan, combine the water and teff and bring to a boil over high heat. Reduce the heat to low, cover, and simmer for 15 minutes, or until the water is absorbed.

Meanwhile, microwave the coconut milk in a microwavable glass measuring cup on high for 45 seconds to 1 minute, or until hot.

Transfer the cooked teff to a blender. Add the warmed coconut milk, banana, maple syrup, cocoa powder, vanilla, ginger, cloves, and salt. Blend for 3 to 5 minutes, or until smooth.

Serve immediately, topping each serving with a sprinkle of hazelnuts and crystallized ginger.

NUTRITION PER SERVING: 180 calories, 34 g carbs, 4 g fiber, 4 g protein, 5 g total fat, 1 g saturated fat, 40 mg sodium

# 4

# SALADS

# SUMMER CORN SALAD

Recipe by PATRICIA WELLS

**MAKES 4 SERVINGS**
**TOTAL TIME: 20 MINUTES**

## Salad

- 2½ ounces smoked bacon, chopped
- 2 ears fresh corn, shucked
- 4 multicolored heirloom tomatoes, chopped
- 1 avocado, cubed
- ½ cup crumbled feta cheese (2 ounces)
- 2 scallions, white parts only, cut into thin rings

## Dressing

- ½ cup low-fat plain yogurt
- 2 tablespoons fresh lemon juice
- ¼ teaspoon salt
- ¼ teaspoon ground black pepper

*When in season, corn is so tender it doesn't even require cooking—just slice it off the cob and toss it in this dish. The vegetable is a rich source of carbs, fiber, and antioxidants. "I love creating a fresh salad with the day's harvest from the market," says longtime runner and cookbook author Patricia Wells. Pair the salad with grilled chicken or fish to make it a perfect recovery meal option.*

Cook the bacon: Heat a large skillet over medium heat. Add the bacon and cook for 5 minutes, or until crisp and golden brown. With a slotted spoon, transfer the bacon to paper towels and blot to absorb any fat.

Cut off a slice at the wide end of the ears of corn. Stand the ears on the cut end and slice off the kernels. Place the kernels in a large bowl. Add the bacon, tomatoes, avocado, feta, and scallions. Set aside.

Make the dressing: In a screw-top jar, combine the yogurt, lemon juice, and salt. Tightly seal the jar with a lid and shake to blend.

Toss the salad with just enough yogurt dressing to coat the ingredients lightly and evenly. Season with the pepper and lightly toss again.

NUTRITION PER SERVING: 238 calories, 22 g carbs, 6 g fiber, 10 g protein, 14 g total fat, 4.5 g saturated fat, 396 mg sodium

# WHOLE GRAIN PANZANELLA

Recipe by THE RODALE TEST KITCHEN

**MAKES 4 SERVINGS**
**TOTAL TIME: 25 MINUTES**

- 3 cups cubed (½-inch) crusty whole grain bread
- ⅓ cup extra-virgin olive oil
- 2 tablespoons white balsamic vinegar, white wine vinegar, or champagne vinegar
- ½ teaspoon salt
- ¼ teaspoon Dijon mustard
- 1 pound red tomatoes, cut into 1-inch chunks
- ½ pound yellow tomatoes, cut into 1-inch chunks
- 1 small English (seedless) cucumber, halved lengthwise and thinly sliced crosswise
- 1 small red onion, halved and thinly sliced
- ¾ cup packed fresh basil leaves, torn
- ¼ cup pitted gaeta or kalamata olives, halved

*Originally intended as a way to use up stale bread, panzanella (Italian bread salad) has come into its own. By all means, if you've got stale bread, use it here (though still toast it to ensure there aren't any moist spots). It's a hearty salad that could even work as a light lunch by itself or paired with a cup of soup.*

Preheat the oven to 250°F.

Place the bread on a baking sheet and bake for 10 to 15 minutes, or until dried out.

Meanwhile, in a large bowl, whisk together the oil, vinegar, salt, and mustard. Add the red and yellow tomatoes, cucumber, onion, basil, olives, and bread cubes. Toss well.

Serve immediately or set aside for flavors to meld, if desired, for about 10 minutes.

NUTRITION PER SERVING: 352 calories, 25 g carbs, 5 g fiber, 7 g protein, 26 g total fat, 3.5 g saturated fat, 754 mg sodium

QUICK TIP Feel free to add cut-up bell pepper, drained capers, drained white beans or chickpeas, or even some cheese to this recipe.

# JICAMA SLAW

Recipe by MATTHEW KADEY, M.S., R.D.

**MAKES 4 SERVINGS**
**TOTAL TIME: 10 MINUTES**

- 1 cup shredded jicama (from an 8- to 10-ounce jicama)
- 1 cup preshredded red cabbage
- 2 tablespoons chopped walnuts
- 2 tablespoons mayonnaise
- 1 tablespoon apple cider vinegar
- ¼ teaspoon ground black pepper
- ¼ teaspoon celery salt
- ⅛ teaspoon salt

*The crispy flesh of jicama tastes like a cross between cucumber, pear, and water chestnut. One cup sliced contains only 46 calories and is a good source of fiber—6 grams per cup—and vitamin C, which is essential for the body to make the healthy collagen found in tendons and ligaments. Select only firm, dry jicama roots and slice off the thin, dust-brown skin with a vegetable peeler before preparation.*

In a medium bowl, combine the jicama, cabbage, and walnuts.

In a small bowl, combine the mayonnaise, vinegar, pepper, celery salt, and salt until smooth.

Add the mayonnaise mixture to the jicama mixture and toss well to evenly coat. For a crisp slaw with more crunch, serve immediately, or allow to sit for 20 minutes for the flavors to meld.

NUTRITION PER SERVING: 42 calories, 5 g carbs, 2 g fiber, 1 g protein, 2 g total fat, 0 g saturated fat, 141 mg sodium

QUICK TIP Unlike many other root vegetables, jicama is best consumed raw. Shredding jicama with a box grater is an easy way to add it to sandwiches and salads.

# FENNEL POTATO SALAD

Recipe by LIZ APPLEGATE, PH.D.

**MAKES 6 SERVINGS**
**TOTAL TIME: 30 MINUTES**

- 2 pounds small red potatoes, quartered
- ¾ teaspoon salt
- 2 tablespoons extra-virgin olive oil
- 2 teaspoons balsamic vinegar
- ½ teaspoon Dijon mustard
- 2 tablespoons mayonnaise
- 3 scallions, thinly sliced
- 2 stalks celery, diced
- ¼ fennel bulb, diced
- ¼ cup fresh flat-leaf parsley, chopped
- ¼ teaspoon ground black pepper, plus more to taste

*Fennel livens up traditional potato salad, adding crunch, a hint of licorice, and loads of antioxidants. Try this salad for a prerun carb boost.*

In a medium pot, combine the potatoes and cold water to cover. Bring to a boil over high heat. When the water boils, add ¼ teaspoon of the salt, cover the pot, and continue to cook for 6 to 8 minutes, or until a knife easily pierces the potatoes.

Meanwhile, in a large bowl, whisk together the oil, vinegar, and mustard. Whisk in the mayonnaise, then stir in the scallions, celery, fennel, parsley, remaining ½ teaspoon salt, and pepper. Stir well to combine.

Drain the potatoes and add to the bowl. Mix gently until well combined.

NUTRITION PER SERVING: 168 calories, 26 g carbs, 3 g fiber, 3 g protein, 6 g total fat, 1 g saturated fat, 172 mg sodium

# WARM TOMATO, OLIVE, AND ARUGULA SALAD

### Recipe by THE RODALE TEST KITCHEN

**MAKES 4 SERVINGS**
**TOTAL TIME: 25 MINUTES**

- 6 cups baby arugula (about 5 ounces)
- 3 tablespoons balsamic vinegar
- ½ pound green beans
- 1 tablespoon extra-virgin olive oil
- 1 red onion, sliced into thin rings
- ¼ cup pitted kalamata olives, halved
- 6 plum tomatoes, cut into wedges
- ¾ teaspoon fresh thyme leaves or ¼ teaspoon dried
- ¼ teaspoon salt
- ¼ teaspoon ground black pepper
- ¼ cup shaved Parmesan cheese

*Juicy tomatoes, salty olives, and peppery arugula make for a flavor-packed salad. Pair it with a cup of soup or fresh baguette for a complete meal.*

Place the arugula on a large platter and set aside.

In a small saucepan, bring the balsamic vinegar to a simmer over medium-high heat. Simmer for about 1 minute, or until reduced by half and syrupy. Set aside.

Fill a large bowl with ice and water. Fill a large skillet with 2 inches of water and bring to a boil over high heat. Add the green beans, cover, and boil for about 3 minutes, or until the beans are bright green and just tender. Drain the beans in a colander and transfer them to the bowl of ice water for 1 minute. Drain the beans again.

In the same large skillet, heat the olive oil over medium-high heat. Add the onion and olives. Cook, stirring often, for 4 minutes, or until the onion is soft.

Add the green beans, tomatoes, and thyme. Cook, stirring often, for 2 minutes, or just until hot (the tomatoes should remain firm). Remove from the heat and season with the salt and pepper.

Place the cooked vegetables on top of the arugula. Sprinkle with the Parmesan and drizzle with the reduced balsamic.

NUTRITION PER SERVING: 162 calories, 15 g carbs, 4 g fiber, 4 g protein, 10 g total fat, 2 g saturated fat, 548 mg sodium

# SWEET POTATO-PUMPKIN SEED SALAD

### Recipe by MARK BITTMAN

**MAKES 6 SERVINGS**
**TOTAL TIME: 20 MINUTES**

- ¾ cup salted roasted pumpkin seeds
- 1 teaspoon plus a dash of chili powder
- 1 tablespoon plus ¼ cup extra-virgin olive oil
- 2 or 3 sweet potatoes (1¼ pounds total), peeled and grated
- 2 tablespoons red wine vinegar
- 1 tablespoon Dijon mustard
- 2 teaspoons honey
- ¼ cup raisins

*This lightly cooked fall salad from* Runner's World *contributing food writer Mark Bittman offers a wonderful variety of flavors and textures, thanks to the sautéed sweet potatoes, crunchy pumpkin seeds, and sweet chewy raisins. Chili powder provides just a touch of spice that enhances the whole dish.*

Preheat the oven to 375°F. Coat a baking sheet with cooking spray.

Spread the seeds on the baking sheet and sprinkle with 1 teaspoon of the chili powder. Roast for 5 minutes, or until lightly browned. Set aside to cool.

Meanwhile, in a skillet, heat 1 tablespoon of the oil over medium-high heat. Add the sweet potatoes and lightly cook for 7 minutes.

In a bowl, whisk together the vinegar, mustard, honey, and the dash of chili powder. Whisk in the remaining ¼ cup oil. Add the sweet potatoes, pumpkin seeds, and raisins. Toss well.

NUTRITION PER SERVING: 255 calories, 19 g carbs, 2 g fiber, 5 g protein, 19 g total fat, 3 g saturated fat, 113 mg sodium

# SPRING LETTUCES WITH STRAWBERRIES AND FETA

Recipe by THE RODALE TEST KITCHEN

**MAKES 4 SERVINGS**
**TOTAL TIME: 20 MINUTES**

*Any type of fresh, young, spring lettuces or greens will work well in this recipe. Frozen edamame is a convenient way to add protein, but if you can find fresh, in-season peas or fava beans they would make a delicious substitute. Any leftover dressing will keep in the refrigerator for up to a week. Use it on salad greens, potato salad, or pasta salad.*

## Vinaigrette

- 3 tablespoons sherry vinegar or white wine vinegar
- 1 teaspoon minced shallot
- ½ teaspoon Dijon mustard
- ¼ teaspoon salt
  Pinch of ground black pepper
- ⅔ cup extra-virgin olive oil

## Salad

- 1 cup frozen shelled edamame
- ¼ cup sliced almonds
- 6 cups spring lettuces or any spring greens
- ½ cup chopped mixed fresh herbs, such as chives, chervil, and mint
- ½ cup crumbled feta cheese (2 ounces)
- ½ cup sliced strawberries

Make the vinaigrette: In a small bowl, whisk together the vinegar, shallot, mustard, salt, and pepper. While whisking constantly, slowly drizzle in the oil.

For the salad: Cook the edamame according to the package directions. Drain and rinse under cold water to cool.

Heat a skillet over medium heat. Add the almonds and toast for 3 to 5 minutes, until lightly browned.

In a large bowl, combine the lettuces, herbs, feta, strawberries, and almonds.

Add the cooled edamame, drizzle with the vinaigrette, and gently toss to coat.

NUTRITION PER SERVING: 300 calories, 10 g carbs, 4 g fiber, 9 g protein, 26 g total fat, 5.5 g saturated fat, 376 mg sodium

QUICK TIP For an even heartier meal, toss in 1 cup cubed cooked chicken.

# GAZPACHO CHICKEN SALAD

Recipe by MATTHEW KADEY, M.S., R.D.

**MAKES 6 SERVINGS**
**TOTAL TIME: 20 MINUTES**

### Vinaigrette

- ⅓ cup extra-virgin olive oil
- ⅔ cup fresh basil, chopped
- 2 tablespoons red wine vinegar
- ¼ teaspoon salt
- ¼ teaspoon ground black pepper

### Salad

- 1 cucumber
- 4 cups shredded rotisserie chicken
- 2 peaches, chopped
- 1 pint cherry tomatoes, halved
- 1 yellow bell pepper, sliced
- ½ cup diced red onion
- 2 cups cubed day-old baguette or any stale bread or croutons
- 1 cup crumbled feta cheese (4 ounces)
- 6 cups mixed baby greens (about 4 ounces)

*Inspired by the chilled Spanish soup, this vegetable-packed salad contains a wide range of vitamins, minerals, and antioxidants that runners need to recover. Tossing in chicken boosts the protein content, while peaches add a hint of sweetness.*

Make the vinaigrette: In a small bowl, whisk together the oil, basil, vinegar, salt, and pepper.

For the salad: Using a vegetable peeler, shave the cucumber into long strips, stopping at the seedy core. Squeeze out any excess water. In a large bowl, combine the cucumber, chicken, peaches, tomatoes, bell pepper, onion, bread cubes, and feta. Toss well.

Divide the mixed greens among 6 plates. Top each with a portion of the chicken mixture. Drizzle each serving with the dressing.

NUTRITION PER SERVING: 430 calories, 24 g carbs, 4 g fiber, 34 g protein, 23 g total fat, 7 g saturated fat, 842 mg sodium

# SHORTCUT THAI BEEF SALAD

### Recipe by MELISSA LASHER

**MAKES 4 SERVINGS**
**TOTAL TIME: 10 MINUTES**

## Dressing

Juice of 2 limes

4 teaspoons soy sauce

4 teaspoons toasted sesame oil

¼ teaspoon red pepper flakes

## Salad

4 cups prewashed and cut romaine hearts (about 4 ounces)

4 cups preshredded red cabbage (about 10 ounces)

1 cup chopped mixed fresh herbs, such as basil, cilantro, and parsley

2 scallions, thinly sliced

8 ounces deli roast beef, sliced or torn into strips

¼ cup salted peanuts, roughly chopped

*Sliced roast beef is one food you can feel good about buying from the deli counter. Naturally lean and minimally processed, it provides 14 grams of protein per 2-ounce serving. If you have more time to cook, you can substitute grilled strip steak: Grill a 1-inch-thick steak over direct heat for about 8 minutes total, for medium-rare, and allow to rest 5 minutes before slicing across the grain.*

Make the dressing: In a small bowl, whisk together the lime juice, soy sauce, sesame oil, and pepper flakes.

For the salad: In a large bowl, combine the romaine, cabbage, herbs, and scallions. Drizzle the dressing over the greens. Toss well to evenly coat.

Divide the greens among 4 plates. Top each serving with the roast beef and sprinkle with the peanuts.

NUTRITION PER SERVING: 185 calories, 8 g carbs, 3 g fiber, 15 g protein, 11 g total fat, 2 g saturated fat, 684 mg sodium

**QUICK TIP** Look for bags of preshredded cabbage near other leafy greens in the produce aisle.

# BLACK BEAN AND BACON POTATO SALAD

Recipe by MELISSA LASHER

**MAKES 4 SERVINGS**
**TOTAL TIME: 30 MINUTES**

- 1 pound red potatoes, cut into ½-inch cubes
- ¾ teaspoon salt
- 4 slices bacon
- 1 teaspoon chopped shallot
- 1 teaspoon Dijon mustard
- 3 tablespoons white wine vinegar
- ¼ teaspoon ground black pepper
- ¼ teaspoon ground cumin
- ¼ cup extra-virgin olive oil
- 1 can (15 ounces) spicy black beans, drained and lightly rinsed
- 1 cup roughly chopped fresh flat-leaf parsley
- 6 cups mixed baby greens (about 4 ounces)

*Potatoes should be a staple in every runner's kitchen. They're inexpensive, long-lasting, and despite their reputation as being nutrient-poor, they're rich in carbs, fiber, vitamin C, and potassium. Adding a bit of flavorful bacon and protein-packed black beans transforms simple spuds into a full meal.*

In a medium pot, combine the potatoes with cold water to cover. Bring to a boil over high heat. When the water boils, add ¼ teaspoon of the salt, cover the pot, and continue to cook for 2 to 4 minutes, or until a knife easily pierces the potatoes.

Meanwhile, heat a skillet over medium-high heat. Add the bacon and cook, flipping halfway through, for 5 minutes, or until crisp. Transfer to a plate lined with paper towels. Set aside.

In a small bowl, whisk together the shallot, mustard, vinegar, pepper, cumin, and remaining ½ teaspoon salt. While continuing to whisk, slowly pour in the oil. Whisk until well combined.

Drain the potatoes in a colander and transfer them to a large serving bowl. Add the beans. Crumble the bacon over top. Add the parsley. Drizzle with 3 tablespoons of the dressing and toss well to coat. Dress the greens with the remaining dressing.

Divide the greens among 4 plates. Top with a portion of the potato salad.

**NUTRITION PER SERVING:** 316 calories, 33 g carbs, 8 g fiber, 11 g protein, 18 g total fat, 3 g saturated fat, 611 mg sodium

# STEAK AND PEACH SALAD

Recipe by MATTHEW KADEY, M.S., R.D.

**MAKES 4 SERVINGS**
**TOTAL TIME: 25 MINUTES**

## Dressing

- ¼ cup canola oil
- 1½ tablespoons balsamic vinegar
- 2 teaspoons unsweetened cocoa powder
- 1 tablespoon honey
- 2 teaspoons Dijon mustard
- ¼ teaspoon salt
- ¼ teaspoon chili powder

## Salad

- 1 pound flank steak
- ½ teaspoon salt
- ½ teaspoon ground black pepper
- 3 peaches, halved
- 1 teaspoon canola oil
- 6 cups baby spinach (about 5 ounces)
- 1 cucumber, chopped
- 1 red bell pepper, sliced
- ¼ cup crumbled feta cheese (1 ounce)
- ¼ cup chopped fresh mint

*Meaty steak, juicy peaches, and a cocoa and chili infused dressing may seem like an unusual combination, but they provide an irresistible mix of textures and flavors that balance each other perfectly. With 2 grams of fat per ounce, flank is one of the leaner steak options, and it's rich in muscle-building protein and iron.*

Preheat a grill or grill pan on high heat.

Meanwhile, make the dressing: In a small bowl, whisk together the oil, vinegar, cocoa powder, honey, mustard, salt, and chili powder in a small bowl. Set aside.

For the salad: Season both sides of the flank steak with the salt and pepper and put it on the grill. Cook for 6 to 8 minutes, flipping the steak halfway through, until both sides are browned and show grill marks. Remove the steak to a cutting board and let it rest, covered, for 5 minutes, then thinly slice against the grain.

Meanwhile, reduce the grill heat to medium. Brush the peach halves with the oil and grill, cut sides down, for 3 minutes. Flip and grill 1 minute longer. Cut into wedges.

Divide the spinach among 4 plates. Top with equal amounts of steak, peaches, cucumber, bell pepper, feta, and mint. Drizzle with the dressing.

NUTRITION PER SERVING: 447 calories, 25 g carbs, 5 g fiber, 29 g protein, 27 g total fat, 7 g saturated fat, 723 mg sodium

QUICK TIP Remove the steak from the fridge (so that it comes to room temperature) and get the grill preheating before you begin prepping to speed cooking along.

# SHRIMP AND ASPARAGUS SALAD WITH CARROT DRESSING

Recipe by MATTHEW KADEY, M.S., R.D.

**MAKES 4 SERVINGS**
**TOTAL TIME: 30 MINUTES**

*Rich in complex carbs, whole grain bulgur is the perfect addition to any salad the night before a long run. Shrimp is low in fat and calories but provides plenty of protein and selenium, an antioxidant that may help protect against cell-damaging oxidative stress linked to exercise.*

## Salad

- 1 cup medium-grind (#2) whole grain bulgur
- 2 cups low-sodium vegetable broth, warmed
- 1 pound cooked medium shrimp, peeled
- 2 teaspoons extra-virgin olive oil
- 1 bunch asparagus (1 pound), trimmed and cut crosswise into 2-inch pieces
- ⅓ cup chopped almonds
- ¼ cup slivered or chopped oil-packed sun-dried tomatoes, well drained

## Dressing

- ¼ cup carrot juice
- 2 tablespoons almond or walnut oil
- 1 tablespoon white wine vinegar
- Grated zest of 1 lemon
- 1 small clove garlic, minced
- ½ teaspoon ground cumin
- ¼ teaspoon salt
- ¼ teaspoon ground black pepper

Cook the bulgur: Heat a saucepan over medium heat. Add the bulgur and toast for 2 to 3 minutes, or until aromatic, shaking the pan often. Add the broth and bring to a simmer. Cover and cook for 10 to 12 minutes, or until tender.

Meanwhile, make the dressing: In a bowl, whisk together the carrot juice, almond oil, vinegar, lemon zest, garlic, cumin, salt, and pepper. Set aside.

For the salad: Drain the bulgur if necessary and transfer it to a large bowl, then fluff with a fork. Add the shrimp and stir gently to incorporate. Set aside.

In a large skillet, heat the olive oil over medium heat. Add the asparagus and cook for 5 minutes, or until crisp-tender.

Add the asparagus to the bulgur bowl, along with the almonds and sun-dried tomatoes. Drizzle with the dressing and toss to combine.

NUTRITION PER SERVING: 418 calories, 36 g carbs, 10 g fiber, 36 g protein, 16 g total fat, 1.5 g saturated fat, 377 mg sodium

QUICK TIP You can also make this salad with whole wheat couscous or quinoa.

# QUINOA-KALE SALAD WITH FRESH APRICOTS

Recipe by PAM ANDERSON

**MAKES 4 SERVINGS**
**TOTAL TIME: 30 MINUTES**

### Salad

- 1 cup quinoa
- 2 cups water
- 4 cups prewashed chopped kale
- 1 can (15 ounces) kidney beans, drained and rinsed
- 1½ cups diced fresh apricots (about 4 medium) or 1 cup dried apricots, diced
- ¼ red onion, roughly chopped
- ¼ cup fresh cilantro leaves

### Dressing

- ⅓ cup low-fat plain kefir
- 1½ tablespoons whole grain Dijon mustard
- 2 cloves garlic, minced
- 1 teaspoon ground cumin
- ⅛ teaspoon ground black pepper
- Pinch of salt
- 3 tablespoons extra-virgin olive oil

Runner's World *contributing chef Pam Anderson pulls together what she calls an "über-superfood salad" that's perfect for summer barbecues.*

Cook the quinoa: Heat a large saucepan or small Dutch oven over medium heat. Add the quinoa and toast about 2 minutes, or until fragrant and slightly darker in color. Add the water, cover, and bring to a simmer. Reduce the heat to medium-low and simmer for 12 to 15 minutes, until the water is absorbed and the quinoa is fully cooked. Uncover, fluff with a fork, and spread the quinoa on a plate to cool to lukewarm.

Meanwhile, make the dressing: In a small bowl, whisk together the kefir, mustard, garlic, cumin, pepper, and salt. Slowly whisk in oil to make a thick dressing.

For the salad: Place the kale, beans, apricots, onion, and cilantro in a large bowl. Add the quinoa and the dressing. Toss to coat.

NUTRITION PER SERVING: 390 calories, 53 g carbs, 9 g fiber, 15 g protein, 14 g fat, 2 g saturated fat, 290 mg sodium

# GREEN AND WHITE BEAN SALAD WITH TUNA

### Recipe by PAM ANDERSON

**MAKES 4 SERVINGS**
**TOTAL TIME: 20 MINUTES**

¼ teaspoon salt

½ pound green beans, halved

2 cans (5 to 6 ounces each) water-packed albacore tuna, drained

1 can (15 ounces) white beans, drained and rinsed

1 can (2.25 ounces) sliced black olives

¼ red onion, cut into thin slivers

1 teaspoon dried oregano

¼ cup extra-virgin olive oil

½ teaspoon grated lemon zest

2 tablespoons fresh lemon juice

4 hard-boiled eggs

*"Lunch for me is usually soup or salad," says* Runner's World *contributing chef Pam Anderson. "But it has to be substantial, like this Niçoise-inspired plate." Save some time by buying precooked hard-boiled eggs at the salad bar or deli section in the supermarket. Look for pole-and-line caught canned albacore tuna at the supermarket. It is lower in mercury than conventionally fished albacore.*

Fill a large bowl with ice and water. Fill a medium saucepan with 2 inches of water and bring to a boil over high heat. Add the salt, followed by the green beans. Cover and boil for 4 minutes, or until the beans are bright green and just tender. Drain the beans in a colander and transfer them to the bowl of ice water for 1 minute. Drain the beans again. Set aside.

In a large bowl, combine the tuna, white beans, olives, onion, oregano, oil, lemon zest, and lemon juice. Toss well to combine.

Divide the green beans among 4 plates. Top each with an even portion of the tuna salad and 1 egg.

NUTRITION PER SERVING: 402 calories, 22 g carbs, 5 g fiber, 26 g protein, 24 g total fat, 4 g saturated fat, 405 mg sodium

QUICK TIP You can also make this salad using canned sardines instead of the tuna. Sardines have a stronger flavor but are ecofriendly and rich in omega-3 fatty acids.

# CREAMY AVOCADO DRESSING

Recipe by THE RODALE TEST KITCHEN

**MAKES 1 CUP**
**TOTAL TIME: 5 MINUTES**

- 1 avocado
- ½ cup water
- Juice of 1 lemon
- ¼ cup fresh cilantro leaves
- ¼ teaspoon salt
- ¼ teaspoon ground cumin (optional)
- 1 small clove garlic

*You'll never buy bottled creamy dressing again after tasting this super simple avocado dressing, which adds rich flavor to everyday salads without actually using any cream. It's also delicious added to pasta salads.*

In a blender, combine the avocado, water, lemon juice, cilantro, salt, cumin (if using), and garlic. Blend until smooth, adding more water by the tablespoon, as necessary, to thin to desired consistency.

NUTRITION PER 2-TABLESPOON SERVING: 42 calories, 3 g carbs, 2 g fiber, 1 g protein, 4 g total fat, 0.5 g saturated fat, 75 mg sodium

# DIJON LEMON VINAIGRETTE

Recipe by THE RODALE TEST KITCHEN

**MAKES ½ CUP**
**TOTAL TIME: 5 MINUTES**

- 2 tablespoons fresh lemon juice
- 1 tablespoon white wine vinegar
- 2 teaspoons Dijon mustard
- ¼ teaspoon salt
- ¼ teaspoon ground black pepper
- 6 tablespoons extra-virgin olive oil

*Bright and tangy, this dressing livens up even the most basic of salads. Store any extra in the refrigerator for up to a week.*

In a small bowl, whisk together the lemon juice, vinegar, mustard, salt, and pepper. Slowly whisk in the oil until well combined.

NUTRITION PER 2-TABLESPOON SERVING: 181 calories, 1 g carbs, 0 g fiber, 0 g protein, 20 g total fat, 3 g saturated fat, 178 mg sodium

Spicy Miso Dressing,
opposite page

Dijon Lemon
Vinaigrette, page 99

Fresh Herb Vinaigrette,
opposite page

Creamy Avocado
Dressing, page 99

# SPICY MISO DRESSING

Recipe by THE RODALE TEST KITCHEN

**MAKES A GENEROUS ½ CUP**
**TOTAL TIME: 10 MINUTES**

- 1 tablespoon wasabi powder
- 2 tablespoons water
- 2 tablespoons white (shiro) miso paste
- ¼ cup lime juice (about 2 limes)
- 1 tablespoon toasted sesame oil
- 1 tablespoon honey
- ½ teaspoon salt
- ½ teaspoon grated fresh ginger or ground ginger

*This dressing gets a kick from the combination of wasabi and fresh ginger. It's delicious on sturdy salad greens, as well as Asian noodles. For an extra-spicy dressing, add an additional tablespoon wasabi powder, or to taste.*

In a medium bowl, stir together the wasabi powder and water to form a paste. Stir in the miso.

Whisk in the lime juice, sesame oil, honey, salt, and ginger until smooth.

NUTRITION PER 2-TABLESPOON SERVING: 71 calories, 10 g carbs, 1 g fiber, 1 g protein, 4 g total fat, 0.5 g saturated fat, 531 mg sodium

# FRESH HERB VINAIGRETTE

Recipe by THE RODALE TEST KITCHEN

**MAKES ABOUT ⅔ CUP**
**TOTAL TIME: 5 MINUTES**

- ⅓ cup extra-virgin olive oil
- ¼ cup balsamic or red wine vinegar
- ½ teaspoon Dijon mustard
- ¼ teaspoon salt
- 2 tablespoons minced fresh herb, such as chives, tarragon, rosemary, parsley, or a combination

*You can make this basic vinaigrette with any combination of fresh herbs. Balsamic vinegar gives it a sweet-yet-tangy flavor that's perfect on mixed greens.*

In a medium screw-top jar, combine the oil, vinegar, mustard, and salt. Cover and shake until well combined. Add the herbs and shake again.

NUTRITION PER 2-TABLESPOON SERVING: 140 calories, 2 g carbs, 0 g fiber, 0 g protein, 14 g total fat, 2 g saturated fat, 132 mg sodium

# 5

# SOUPS and STEWS

# COLD AVOCADO AND CRAB SOUP

Recipe by MATTHEW KADEY, M.S., R.D.

**MAKES 4 SERVINGS**
**TOTAL TIME: 20 MINUTES**

- 2½ cups unsweetened coconut water
- 2 avocados
- 2 cups baby spinach
- ½ English (seedless) cucumber, chopped
- ¼ cup fresh basil leaves
- Juice of 1 lime, plus 1 teaspoon grated zest
- 1 tablespoon honey
- 1 jalapeño, seeded and chopped (wear gloves while handling)
- 1 clove garlic, chopped
- ¼ teaspoon salt
- ¼ teaspoon ground black pepper
- 6 ounces pasteurized lump or backfin crabmeat
- 1 mango, cubed
- 1 red bell pepper, diced

*Coconut water forms the base of this chilled soup, providing lightly sweet and nutty flavor along with potassium, which helps regulate muscle contractions and your heartbeat. Avocado creates a silky texture while providing cholesterol-lowering fiber and monounsaturated fat, plus vitamin C. Research shows that vitamin C may reduce your heart rate during exercise and make runs seem less taxing. If you have the time, chill all the ingredients beforehand.*

In a blender, combine the coconut water, avocados, spinach, cucumber, basil, lime juice, honey, jalapeño, garlic, salt, and black pepper. Blend until smooth.

In a bowl, combine the crabmeat, mango, bell pepper, and lime zest. Toss well. Serve immediately or chill both the soup and crab mixture, covered, until ready to serve.

Ladle the soup into bowls and top with the crab mixture.

NUTRITION PER SERVING: 316 calories, 38 g carbs, 10 g fiber, 12 g protein, 15 g total fat, 2.5 g saturated fat, 370 mg sodium

QUICK TIP For more spice, swap in a serrano chile for the jalapeño.

# HONEYDEW SOUP

Recipe by AMY FRITCH

**MAKES 4 SERVINGS**
**TOTAL TIME: 10 MINUTES**

- 1 honeydew melon, cut into chunks
- ½ cup 2% plain Greek yogurt
- 2 tablespoons fresh mint leaves
- ½ teaspoon vanilla extract
- 1 to 2 tablespoons agave syrup (optional)
- 1 tablespoon unsweetened flaked coconut

*Sweet and juicy, honeydew forms the base of this cold, refreshing soup. A touch of yogurt adds creaminess without weighing you down before a run.*

In a blender or food processor, combine the honeydew, yogurt, mint, and vanilla and process until smooth. Taste for sweetness and add the agave syrup, if desired. Ladle the soup into 4 bowls and top with flaked coconut.

NUTRITION PER SERVING: 149 calories, 31 g carbs, 3 g fiber, 5 g protein, 2 g total fat, 1 g saturated fat, 72 mg sodium

QUICK TIP You can substitute other summer fruit, such as cantaloupe, strawberries, raspberries, or peaches, for the honeydew.

# MINESTRONE VERDE

Recipe by THE RODALE TEST KITCHEN

**MAKES 4 SERVINGS**
**TOTAL TIME: 30 MINUTES**

- 1 tablespoon extra-virgin olive oil
- 1 medium leek, halved lengthwise, well rinsed, and thinly sliced (including some green tops)
- 2 large stalks celery, thinly sliced
- 3 cloves garlic, minced
- ½ teaspoon dried oregano
- ¼ teaspoon ground black pepper
- ¼ teaspoon salt
- 4 cups reduced-sodium chicken broth
- 4 cups chopped Swiss chard leaves, ribs removed
- ⅔ cup frozen baby lima beans
- ½ cup ditalini or orzo pasta
- 1 piece (2 inches) Parmesan rind (optional)
- ¼ cup chopped fresh flat-leaf parsley
- ½ cup frozen green peas
- 4 teaspoons shredded Parmesan cheese

*With its vibrant green color, this soup is as beautiful—and delicious—as it is healthy. And it's easily customized. You can substitute another green option for any of the herbs or vegetables listed in the ingredients. And while they're not green, canned diced tomatoes are also a delicious addition to the soup.*

In a large soup pot, heat the oil over medium heat. Add the leek, celery, garlic, oregano, pepper, and salt. Cook, stirring frequently, for 4 minutes, or until the vegetables begin to soften.

Add the broth, Swiss chard, lima beans, pasta, and Parmesan rind (if using). Increase the heat and bring to a boil. Reduce the heat to medium-low, cover, and simmer for 8 minutes, or until the vegetables are tender and the pasta is cooked.

Stir the parsley and peas into the soup. Cover and cook for 2 minutes longer, or until the peas are heated through. (Remove the Parmesan rind and discard.)

Ladle the soup into 4 bowls and top each with 1 teaspoon shredded Parmesan.

NUTRITION PER SERVING: 181 calories, 26 g carbs, 4 g fiber, 10 g protein, 5 g total fat, 1 g saturated fat, 861 mg sodium

**QUICK TIP** After grating a wedge of Parmesan down to the rind, don't throw it away. Save it to add to soups like this one. It's full of savory flavor and helps add depth to vegetarian soups.

# CHILLED GOLDEN ZUCCHINI AND BUTTERMILK SOUP

### Recipe by PATRICIA WELLS

**MAKES 4 SERVINGS**
**TOTAL TIME: 10 MINUTES**

- 1 or 2 large cloves garlic, halved
- 1 pound golden zucchini or yellow summer squash, chopped
- 1 teaspoon salt
- 2 cups reduced-fat buttermilk, shaken to blend
- ¼ cup minced fresh dill or mint (or a combination)

*Soups do not get simpler, healthier, or more satisfying than this. It's delicious after a hot summer run—and it can be prepared in a snap. Pair it with Warm Tomato, Olive, and Arugula Salad (page 82).*

In a food processor or a blender, mince the garlic. Add the zucchini, salt, and buttermilk and process for 1 minute, or until it becomes a smooth liquid. Serve in soup bowls and garnish with the dill or mint. Store (without the garnish) in an airtight container in the refrigerator for up to 3 days. Reblend at serving time.

NUTRITION PER SERVING: 92 calories, 11 g carbs, 1 g fiber, 7 g protein, 3 g total fat, 1.5 g saturated fat; 731 mg sodium

**QUICK TIP** You can use a 1-pound English cucumber in place of the zucchini or summer squash; if you can find zucchini or squash blossoms, slice them into thin strips and use in place of the dill or mint.

# HEARTY MISO SOUP

Recipe by MARK BITTMAN

**MAKES 4 SERVINGS**
**TOTAL TIME: 25 MINUTES**

    6 cups water

    2 medium sweet potatoes,
      peeled and cut into ½-inch
      cubes

    1 small head (about 1 pound)
      napa or Savoy cabbage,
      chopped

    ⅓ cup white (shiro) or
      light yellow miso paste

    1 can (15 ounces) white
      beans, drained and rinsed

    2 scallions, sliced

    2 teaspoons toasted
      sesame oil

*A staple in Japanese cuisine, miso is a fermented soybean paste that adds savory richness to foods. It contains probiotic bacteria that can help promote digestive health. Look for it in the Asian section of most grocery stores.*

In a large pot, bring the water to a boil over medium-high heat. Add the sweet potatoes and cook for 10 minutes, or until tender. Add the cabbage and cook until barely tender, about 1 minute.

In a bowl, whisk together the miso with 1 cup of the cooking water. Return to the pot. Add the beans. Cook on medium until heated through.

Ladle into bowls and garnish with the scallions and sesame oil.

NUTRITION PER SERVING: 223 calories, 40 g carbs, 7 g fiber, 9 g protein, 3 g total fat, 0.5 g saturated fat, 679 mg sodium

QUICK TIP: Miso comes in three basic varieties—white, yellow, and red. The darker the miso, the stronger, saltier, and more pungent it will taste.

# RAINY DAY ONION SOUP

Recipe by THE RODALE TEST KITCHEN

**MAKES 4 SERVINGS**
**TOTAL TIME: 30 MINUTES**

- 3 tablespoons extra-virgin olive oil
- 2 large yellow onions, halved and thinly sliced
- Leaves from 2 sprigs fresh thyme
- 1 bay leaf
- ¼ cup dry sherry
- 2 cans (14 ounces each) reduced-sodium beef broth
- ¼ teaspoon salt
- ¼ teaspoon ground black pepper
- 4 slices (½-inch) whole wheat baguette
- 1 cup shredded Swiss cheese (4 ounces)

*After coming in from a cold, rainy run, nothing is more comforting than a warm bowl of soup. With its rich beef broth, sweet onions, and just the right amount of gooey cheese, this soup will warm you to your core. Most of the actual cooking time in this recipe is spent caramelizing the onions—it's 15 minutes well spent.*

In a large skillet, heat the oil over medium-high heat. Add the onions, thyme, and bay leaf, and cook for 15 minutes, stirring occasionally, until caramelized and very soft.

Add the sherry and scrape up the browned bits from the bottom of the pan. When evaporated, add the broth and bring to a boil. Reduce the heat to low and simmer for 5 minutes. Add the salt and pepper.

Meanwhile, position an oven rack 4 inches from the heat and preheat the broiler to high. Place the bread slices on a baking sheet and top each with 2 tablespoons cheese. Broil for 2½ minutes, or until the bread is toasted and the cheese is golden and melted.

Place 2 tablespoons of cheese in the bottom of each of four 10- or 12-ounce bowls. Remove the bay leaf from the soup and discard. Ladle the hot soup into the bowls. Top each with one slice of cheese toast.

NUTRITION PER SERVING: 300 calories, 16 g carbs, 2 g fiber, 13 g protein, 20 g total fat, 7 g saturated fat, 323 mg sodium

# RED LENTIL SOUP

Recipe by JOANNA SAYAGO GOLUB

**MAKES 4 SERVINGS**
**TOTAL TIME: 25 MINUTES**

- 5 cups reduced-sodium vegetable broth
- 1 cup red lentils
- 1 tablespoon coconut oil or extra-virgin olive oil
- 1 large sweet onion, chopped
- 3 cloves garlic, chopped
- 1 can (14.5 ounces) diced tomatoes
- 1 teaspoon ground cumin
- 1 teaspoon ground coriander
- 1 teaspoon turmeric
- ¼ teaspoon salt

*When it comes to runner-friendly nutrition, lentils are a perfect food. They're high in both carbohydrates and protein and are rich in fiber, which helps keep you full. Lentils are also a good source of iron, which many runners don't get enough of, and provide B vitamins, manganese, and copper. Red lentils (sometimes called by their Indian name* mansoor) *cook faster than green varieties. They also break down as they cook, which gives this recipe a thicker, stew-like consistency.*

In a large soup pot, combine the broth and lentils. Bring to a boil over high heat. Reduce the heat to low and simmer for 10 minutes.

Meanwhile, in a large skillet, heat the oil over medium heat. Add the onion and cook, stirring occasionally, for 4 to 5 minutes, or until softened and translucent. Add the garlic and cook, stirring constantly, for 1 minute, or until fragrant.

After the lentils have cooked for 10 minutes, scrape the onion mixture into the pot. Add the tomatoes (with their juices). Add the cumin, coriander, turmeric, and salt. Stir to combine. Increase the heat slightly to bring the mixture back to a simmer. Allow it to simmer 5 minutes longer, or until the lentils are tender.

NUTRITION PER SERVING: 273 calories, 43 g carbs, 5 g fiber, 14 g protein, 4 g total fat, 3 g saturated fat, 562 mg sodium

# QUICK-COOKING BARLEY AND KALE SOUP

### Recipe by THE RODALE TEST KITCHEN

**MAKES 4 SERVINGS**
**TOTAL TIME: 30 MINUTES**

- 1 tablespoon canola oil
- 1 package (10 to 14 ounces) prediced mirepoix
- ½ pound lean (93%) ground turkey
- 1½ teaspoons poultry seasoning
- ½ teaspoon garlic salt
- ½ teaspoon ground black pepper
- ¾ cup quick-cooking barley
- 5 cups reduced-sodium chicken broth
- 2 cups baby kale leaves
- 4 tablespoons grated Parmesan cheese

*Quick-cooking barley is rolled thinner than traditional pearl barley, so the cooking time is 20 to 30 minutes shorter. Look for it at the supermarket and natural foods stores. Be sure to use lean ground turkey (not ground turkey breast). The former contains dark meat, which helps boost flavor and provides more zinc and iron.*

In a soup pot, heat the oil over medium heat. Add the mirepoix and cook, stirring occasionally, for 5 minutes, or until the vegetables are softened.

Add the turkey, poultry seasoning, garlic salt, and pepper. Cook, breaking the turkey into small chunks, for 3 minutes, or until the meat is no longer pink.

Add the barley and cook, stirring, for 2 minutes. Add the broth, increase the heat to high, and bring to a boil. Reduce the heat to low, add the kale, and simmer for 7 minutes, or until the barley is tender.

Ladle the soup into bowls and sprinkle 1 tablespoon Parmesan over each.

NUTRITION PER SERVING: 288 calories, 31 g carbs, 5 g fiber, 21 g protein, 10 g total fat, 2.5 g saturated fat, 967 mg sodium

**QUICK TIP** Prediced mirepoix (a mixture of onion, carrot, and celery) is just one of many healthy convenience options in the produce section. If you don't have prediced mirepoix, you can instead chop 1 onion, 2 carrots, and 1 stalk celery.

# BLACK AND WHITE BEAN SAUSAGE SOUP

Recipe by LIZ APPLEGATE, PH.D.

**MAKES 6 SERVINGS**
**TOTAL TIME: 30 MINUTES**

- 2 tablespoons extra-virgin olive oil
- 3 cups (14 ounces) prediced mirepoix
- 3 cloves garlic, chopped
- 4 cups reduced-sodium chicken broth
- 2 red potatoes, cut into ½-inch cubes
- ½ pound Italian sausage, casings removed
- 1 can (15 ounces) black beans, drained and rinsed
- 1 can (15 ounces) white beans, drained and rinsed
- 3 tablespoons pesto

*Yes, sausage is high in fat, but here you need just ½ pound of it to create a meaty-tasting soup while still keeping calories in check. Stirring in pesto gives the broth a lovely color and adds richness. Sausage is often gluten-free, but supersensitive runners should check the package to be sure.*

In a 4-quart pot, heat 1 tablespoon of the oil over medium heat. Add the mirepoix and garlic. Cook for 4 to 5 minutes, stirring often, until fragrant and softened.

Add the broth and potatoes, increase the heat to high, and bring to a boil. Reduce the heat to medium-low and simmer for 10 minutes, or until the potatoes are just about soft.

Meanwhile, in a medium skillet, heat the remaining tablespoon oil over medium heat. Add the sausage and cook for 5 to 7 minutes, until no longer pink. Drain well.

To the soup pot, add the sausage, black and white beans, and pesto. Stir to combine. Simmer another 7 to 10 minutes, or until heated through.

NUTRITION PER SERVING: 320 calories, 35 g carbs, 7 g fiber, 18 g protein, 13 g total fat, 3 g saturated fat, 511 mg sodium

QUICK TIP Don't have mirepoix on hand? Substitute 1 diced onion, 2 or 3 diced carrots, and 2 or 3 diced celery stalks.

# STIR-FRY SOUP

**Recipe by JOANNA SAYAGO GOLUB**

**MAKES 6 SERVINGS**
**TOTAL TIME: 20 MINUTES**

- 2 tablespoons light sesame oil or canola oil
- 1 carrot, thinly sliced
- 2 cloves garlic, minced
- 1 tablespoon minced fresh ginger
- 4 cups reduced-sodium vegetable or chicken broth
- 1 package (12 to 14 ounces) extra-firm tofu, drained and cut into ½-inch cubes
- 1 package (3 to 5 ounces) presliced shiitake mushrooms
- 1 bag (5 or 6 ounces) baby spinach
- 2 tablespoons reduced-sodium soy sauce
- 2 scallions, thinly sliced
- ½ teaspoon red pepper flakes (optional)

*No other dish cooks faster than a stir-fry. But the time it takes to prep those vegetables (as well as putting together the laundry list of ingredients needed for a sauce) can often slow you down. A few smart shortcuts (like using presliced mushrooms and cleaned, bagged baby spinach) save you valuable minutes, while a quick simmer in broth replaces the need for complicated sauces.*

In a large wok or soup pot, heat the oil over medium heat. Add the carrot, garlic, and ginger. Cook, stirring frequently, for 3 minutes, or until softened and fragrant.

Increase the heat to high and add the broth, tofu, and mushrooms. Bring to a boil, then reduce the heat to medium-low and add the spinach. Simmer gently for 1 to 2 minutes, or until the spinach is wilted. Stir in the soy sauce.

Ladle the soup into bowls and garnish with the scallions and red pepper flakes, if desired.

NUTRITION PER SERVING: 157 calories, 9 g carbs, 3 g fiber, 11 g protein, 9 g total fat, 1.5 g saturated fat, 289 mg sodium

# CURRIED PUMPKIN SOUP

Recipe by THE RODALE TEST KITCHEN

**MAKES 4 SERVINGS**
**TOTAL TIME: 30 MINUTES**

- 1 tablespoon extra-virgin olive oil
- 1 onion, chopped
- 2 cloves garlic, chopped
- ½ tablespoon grated fresh ginger
- 2½ teaspoons curry powder
- ½ teaspoon ground cumin
- ¼ teaspoon ground cardamom
- 1 can (15 ounces) unsweetened pumpkin puree
- 1 can (14 ounces) light coconut milk
- ½ cup reduced-sodium vegetable or chicken broth
- ½ cup apple cider
- ½ teaspoon salt
- ½ teaspoon ground black pepper
- ¼ cup low-fat plain yogurt
- ¼ cup salted roasted pumpkin seeds
- 1 tablespoon chopped fresh cilantro

*Canned pumpkin puree is a runner-friendly, nutrient-packed shortcut that you can easily cook into a weeknight soup. This recipe shows off pumpkin's savory side. Pair it with Shortcut Thai Beef Salad (page 90) and a loaf of crusty bread for the perfect recovery meal.*

In a large soup pot, heat the oil over medium heat. Add the onion, garlic, and ginger, and cook, stirring frequently, for 5 minutes, or until softened and fragrant.

Add the curry powder, cumin, and cardamom and cook 1 minute longer, stirring to coat. Add the pumpkin puree and coconut milk. Whisk to combine. Pour in the broth and cider and stir. Increase the heat to high and bring to a boil. Reduce the heat to medium-low and simmer for 5 minutes.

Season with the salt and pepper, then transfer to a blender or use an immersion blender to puree until smooth.

Ladle into bowls and swirl in a dollop of yogurt. Garnish with the pumpkin seeds and cilantro.

NUTRITION PER SERVING: 198 calories, 21 g carbs, 5 g fiber, 6 g protein, 11.5 g total fat, 6 g saturated fat, 347 mg sodium

**QUICK TIP** When you're shopping, be sure to buy unsweetened pumpkin puree—not pumpkin pie mix, which contains added sugar and spices.

# SMOKY BLACK BEAN STEW

Recipe by MATTHEW KADEY, M.S., R.D.

**MAKES 4 SERVINGS**
**TOTAL TIME: 30 MINUTES**

- 2 teaspoons canola oil
- 1 onion, diced
- 1 carrot, thinly sliced
- 2 cans (15 ounces each) no-salt-added black beans, drained and rinsed
- 1 can (28 ounces) diced tomatoes
- 1½ cups reduced-sodium vegetable broth
- 1 cup sliced roasted red pepper
- 1 chipotle pepper in adobo sauce, minced
- 1 teaspoon dried thyme
- 1 teaspoon ground cumin
- ¼ teaspoon salt
- ¼ teaspoon ground black pepper
- 1 avocado
- 1 lime
- ¼ cup sour cream (optional)

*Chipotle peppers add deep, smoky flavor to this vegetarian stew, which has the rich flavor of a dish that's simmered on the stove all day—yet takes just 15 minutes to cook. Black beans are high in protein and fiber (1 cup contains 15 grams of both nutrients), which will keep you feeling full and help curb cravings throughout the day. Vegans will want to omit the sour cream used as a topping.*

In a large soup pot, heat the oil over medium-high heat. Add the onion and carrot and cook, stirring occasionally, for 5 minutes, or until softened.

Add the black beans, tomatoes (with their juices), broth, roasted red pepper, chipotle pepper, thyme, cumin, salt, and black pepper. Increase the heat and bring to a boil. Reduce the heat to medium and simmer for 15 minutes, or until thickened and glossy.

Meanwhile, dice the avocado and cut the lime into wedges.

Ladle the stew into bowls and top with the diced avocado and a squeeze of lime. If desired, finish with a dollop of sour cream.

NUTRITION PER SERVING: 277 calories, 42 g carbs, 14 g fiber, 11 g protein, 8 g total fat, 1 g saturated fat, 737 mg sodium

# CHUNKY TOMATO-BEEF SOUP

Recipe by JOANNA SAYAGO GOLUB

**MAKES 6 SERVINGS**
**TOTAL TIME: 30 MINUTES**

- 1 pound ground sirloin
- 1 tablespoon canola oil
- 1 onion, diced
- 1 carrot, diced
- 2 cloves garlic, minced
- 1 can (28 ounces) diced tomatoes
- 4 cups reduced-sodium beef broth
- 2 tablespoons Worcestershire sauce
- ½ teaspoon dried thyme
- 1 cup elbow macaroni or other small pasta
- ¼ teaspoon salt
- ¼ teaspoon ground black pepper
- 2 tablespoons grated Parmesan cheese

*This hearty soup packs recovery-friendly carbs and protein with a good dose of old-school comfort. Meaty and filling without being overly rich, it's perfect after a tough run when you need to refuel but don't want to feel weighed down.*

Heat a large soup pot over medium-high heat. Add the sirloin and cook, breaking the meat into crumbles, for about 3 minutes, or until no longer pink. Transfer it to a bowl and set aside.

Add the oil to the pot. When hot, add the onion and carrot. Cook, stirring frequently, for 3 to 4 minutes, or until the vegetables begin to soften. Add the garlic and cook 30 seconds longer.

Add the tomatoes (with their juices), broth, Worcestershire sauce, beef (along with any juices that accumulated), and thyme. Increase the heat to high and bring the soup to a boil. Stir in the macaroni. Reduce the heat to medium-low and simmer for 8 to 10 minutes, or until the macaroni is tender. Season with the salt and pepper.

Ladle into bowls and serve with a sprinkling of Parmesan.

NUTRITION PER SERVING: 302 calories, 25 g carbs, 2 g fiber, 23 g protein, 12 g total fat, 4 g saturated fat, 580 mg sodium

# SPICY SALMON AND RICE NOODLE SOUP

Recipe by THE RODALE TEST KITCHEN

**MAKES 6 SERVINGS**
**TOTAL TIME: 30 MINUTES**

1 tablespoon canola oil

1 shallot, thinly sliced

1 tablespoon finely grated fresh ginger

1 tablespoon red curry paste

1 can (14 ounces) light coconut milk

4 cups low-sodium vegetable broth

1 package (6 to 7 ounces) rice stick noodles

1 tablespoon fish sauce

1 tablespoon reduced-sodium soy sauce

Juice of 1 lime, plus lime wedges for serving

¾ pound skinless salmon fillet, cut into 1-inch pieces

4 ounces snow peas, halved crosswise

¼ cup chopped fresh cilantro

*This Malaysian soup gets heat from red curry paste, which is available in most supermarkets and Asian grocery stores. The spicy note is perfectly balanced by the cooling coconut milk.*

In a large soup pot, heat the oil over medium heat. Add the shallot and cook for 2 minutes, or until softened. Add the ginger and curry paste and cook for 1 minute. Gradually add the coconut milk and broth. Increase the heat to high and bring to a boil. Reduce the heat to medium and simmer for 10 minutes.

Meanwhile, bring a large pot of water to a boil. Add the noodles and cook for 5 minutes, or just until tender. Drain and rinse in a colander under cold running water. Cover with a damp paper towel and set aside.

Add the fish sauce, soy sauce, lime juice, and salmon to the soup pot. Stir gently. Partially cover and simmer for 5 to 6 minutes, until the fish is cooked through. Add the snow peas and remove from the heat.

If the noodles are sticking together and hard to handle, run them briefly under hot water and drain again.

To serve, place the noodles in deep soup bowls and ladle the soup on top. Garnish with the cilantro and serve with lime wedges.

NUTRITION PER SERVING: 285 calories, 32 g carbs, 2 g fiber, 16 g protein, 11 g total fat, 4 g saturated fat, 572 mg sodium

**QUICK TIP** You can substitute any firm-fleshed fish, such as halibut, mahi-mahi, or striped bass, for the salmon.

# SWEET POTATO CHICKEN STEW

Recipe by JOANNA SAYAGO GOLUB

**MAKES 4 SERVINGS**
**TOTAL TIME: 30 MINUTES**

- 2 tablespoons extra-virgin olive oil
- 1 sweet onion, chopped
- 2 cloves garlic, minced
- 3 cups reduced-sodium chicken broth
- 1 can (14 ounces) petite-diced tomatoes, drained
- 1 can (15 ounces) white beans, such as cannellini or Great Northern, drained and rinsed
- 1 teaspoon smoked paprika
- 2 medium sweet potatoes, peeled and cut into ½-inch cubes
- 2 cups shredded rotisserie chicken (skin removed)
- ¼ teaspoon salt
- ¼ teaspoon ground black pepper
- 2 tablespoons chopped fresh flat-leaf parsley

*Smoked paprika adds a deep, rich flavor to this quick stew, making it taste as if it simmered for hours. This recipe is a perfect way to use up leftover rotisserie chicken (you'll need the equivalent of 2 breasts or about 10 ounces total).*

In a large soup pot, heat the oil over medium-high heat. Add the onion and cook, stirring occasionally, for 3 minutes, or until softened and translucent. Add the garlic and cook 1 minute longer.

Add the broth, tomatoes, beans, and smoked paprika and stir well. Increase the heat to high and bring to a boil. Add the sweet potatoes, cover, reduce the heat to medium, and simmer for 10 minutes, or until the sweet potatoes are tender.

Scoop out 1 cup of stew and carefully transfer to a blender. Puree until smooth. Stir the puree back into the pot. (Alternatively, use an immersion blender to puree some of the soup directly in the pot.) Add the chicken and simmer until the chicken is heated through. Season with the salt and pepper.

Ladle into bowls and garnish with the parsley.

NUTRITION PER SERVING: 344 calories, 34 g carbs, 6 g fiber, 29 g protein, 11 g total fat, 2 g saturated fat, 651 mg sodium

# CREAMY FISH CHOWDER

**Recipe by JENNIFER KUSHNIER**

**MAKES 4 SERVINGS**
**TOTAL TIME: 30 MINUTES**

- 2 cups reduced-sodium vegetable broth or seafood stock
- 8 ounces bottled clam juice
- ¾ pound red or white potatoes, cut into ½-inch dice
- 1 tablespoon extra-virgin olive oil
- 1½ cups (6 ounces) prediced onion and celery mix
- Leaves from 3 sprigs thyme (1½ teaspoons)
- 1 bay leaf
- 4 slices bacon
- 1 pound cod or haddock, cut into 1-inch chunks
- ¼ teaspoon salt
- ¼ teaspoon ground black pepper
- ¾ cup half-and-half, light cream, or milk
- 1 tablespoon snipped fresh chives

*This quick soup has everything a good chowder needs—creamy broth, tender fish, salty bacon, and fresh-herb flavor—without cups of heavy cream and butter to weigh you down. Serve with a crusty bread or the classic pairing, oyster crackers.*

In a medium saucepan, combine the broth, clam juice, and potatoes and bring to a boil over high heat. Reduce the heat to medium to keep the potatoes over a low boil.

Meanwhile, in a medium soup pot, heat the oil over medium-high heat. Add the onion and celery mix, thyme, and bay leaf. Cook, stirring occasionally, for 5 minutes, or until just beginning to soften.

Add the broth mixture and potatoes to the onion and celery and bring to a boil. Reduce the heat to medium and simmer, stirring occasionally, for 10 minutes, or until the potatoes are just tender.

Meanwhile, place the bacon on 2 paper towels on a microwavable plate. Cover with 2 more paper towels. Microwave on high for 1 to 2 minutes, until sizzling. When cool enough to handle, crumble and set aside.

Add the fish, salt, and pepper to the soup pot and simmer for 5 to 7 minutes, or until the fish is cooked through. Remove the bay leaf and discard. Stir in the half-and-half and heat through.

Ladle into bowls and top each with bacon and chives.

NUTRITION PER SERVING: 308 calories, 20 g carbs, 2 g fiber, 27 g protein, 13 g fat, 5 g saturated fat, 595 mg sodium

**QUICK TIP** If you don't want to use prediced onion and celery, dice 2 stalks celery and ½ onion.

# 6

# PASTA and NOODLES

### *Pastas with No-Cook Sauce*

### *Pasta Tosses*

### *Quick Pasta Dinners*

# BOW-TIES WITH TOMATO, BASIL, AND AVOCADO SAUCE

**Recipe by PAM ANDERSON**

**MAKES 4 SERVINGS**
**TOTAL TIME: 25 MINUTES**

- 1 box (12 ounces) whole wheat bow-ties, fusilli, penne, or shells
- 1 pint cherry tomatoes, halved
- ¼ teaspoon salt
- 1 tablespoon extra-virgin olive oil
- ½ cup packed fresh basil leaves, chopped
- 2 avocados
- 3 cloves garlic, chopped
- ¼ cup fresh lemon juice (about 1 large lemon)
- ¼ cup grated Parmesan cheese (optional)
- ¼ teaspoon ground black pepper

*Thanks to its mono- and polyunsaturated fats, avocado gives this pasta dish a heart-healthy richness. When swapped with trans and saturated fats, unsaturated fats reduce levels of LDL, or so-called "bad" cholesterol. Vegan runners should omit the Parmesan.*

Bring a large pot of water to a boil over high heat. When the water boils, salt it and add the bow-ties. Cook according to the package directions.

Meanwhile, put the tomatoes in a small bowl and sprinkle with the salt. Add the oil and basil and toss to coat. Set aside.

Reserving 1 cup of the cooking water, drain the pasta and cover to keep warm. Set aside.

Add the avocados to the empty pasta pot and mash with a potato masher or fork. Add the garlic and lemon juice and stir to combine. Whisk in the reserved pasta cooking water, creating a light sauce. Add the pasta and tomato mixture and toss well to coat. Add the Parmesan (if using) and pepper and toss again.

NUTRITION PER SERVING: 485 calories, 75 g carbs, 13 g fiber, 13 g protein, 16 g total fat, 2 g saturated fat, 231 mg sodium

QUICK TIP All the recipes in this chapter provide a hearty portion of pasta per serving. For a more prerun-friendly meal, simply reduce each portion by about half.

# FETTUCCINE WITH RICOTTA-PISTACHIO SAUCE

Recipe by THE RODALE TEST KITCHEN

**MAKES 6 SERVINGS**
**TOTAL TIME: 25 MINUTES**

- ⅔ cup part-skim ricotta cheese
- ½ cup salted pistachios
- ¼ cup extra-virgin olive oil
- ⅓ cup 1% milk
- ¼ cup roughly chopped fresh flat-leaf parsley, plus more for garnish
- 1 clove garlic, chopped
- ¼ teaspoon salt
  Pinch of ground nutmeg
- 1 box (1 pound) fettuccine or tagliatelle

*Creamy and nutty, this sauce is a cinch to pull together. Just blend up the ingredients while waiting for your pasta water to boil. Pistachios provide heart-healthy fats and essential minerals, while ricotta adds whey protein, which is ideal for jumpstarting muscle recovery.*

Bring a large pot of water to a boil over high heat.

While waiting for the water to boil, in a food processor, combine the ricotta, pistachios, oil, milk, parsley, garlic, salt, and nutmeg and process for 1 minute, or until smooth.

When the water boils, salt it and add the fettuccine. Cook according to the package directions. Reserving ½ cup of the cooking water, drain the pasta in a colander and return it to the pot.

Add the ½ cup pasta cooking water and the sauce to the pasta and toss well to coat.

NUTRITION PER SERVING: 464 calories, 62 g carbs, 4 g fiber, 16 g protein, 17 g fat, 3.5 g saturated fat, 226 mg sodium

# SOBA NOODLES WITH PEANUT-SESAME SAUCE

**Recipe by THE RODALE TEST KITCHEN**

**MAKES 4 SERVINGS**
**TOTAL TIME: 20 MINUTES**

1 package (8 ounces) buckwheat soba noodles

1 cup (3 ounces) snow peas, halved

¼ cup unsweetened smooth peanut butter

¼ cup apple cider vinegar

2 tablespoons soy sauce

2 tablespoons toasted sesame oil

1 clove garlic

¾ teaspoon ground ginger

3 scallions, thinly sliced

1 tablespoon sesame seeds

*You can serve the soba noodles slightly warm or at room temperature. If you make the dish ahead and chill it, let it come to room temperature before serving. You can also use this no-cook peanut-sesame sauce in a stir-fry.*

Bring a large pot of water to a boil over high heat. When the water boils, add the soba noodles. Cook according to the package directions, adding the snow peas during the last minute of cooking.

While the noodles cook, in a food processor, combine the peanut butter, vinegar, soy sauce, sesame oil, garlic, and ginger and process for 30 seconds, or until smooth.

When the noodles are done, drain them along with the peas in a colander and rinse them well under cool water until the water runs clear. Drain well again and return the noodles and peas to the pot. Add the sauce and scallions to the noodles and toss well to coat.

Serve garnished with the sesame seeds.

NUTRITION PER SERVING: 391 calories, 52 g carbs, 2 g fiber, 14 g protein, 17 g total fat, 2 g saturated fat, 952 mg sodium

QUICK TIP While buckwheat is a gluten-free whole grain, many brands of soba noodles are made with wheat as well. Gluten-free runners should be sure to read labels closely.

# SPAGHETTI WITH SUN-DRIED TOMATO SAUCE

**Recipe by NATE APPLEMAN**

**MAKES 6 SERVINGS**
**TOTAL TIME: 25 MINUTES**

- ½ cup almonds
- 1 box (1 pound) spaghetti or bucatini
- 1 cup drained oil-packed sun-dried tomatoes
- ¼ cup extra-virgin olive oil
- 2 anchovy fillets
- 1 clove garlic
- 1 tablespoon chopped fresh basil or 1 teaspoon dried
- ½ teaspoon chopped fresh oregano or a pinch of dried
- 1 teaspoon salt
- 6 tablespoons grated Parmesan cheese

*"This is one of my favorite pastas to make,"* says Runner's World *contributing chef Nate Appleman. "It's fast, easy, and tasty. I like the umami quality that sun-dried tomatoes give any dish. They add so much depth, and the taste just reminds you of the summer—no matter what time of year it is."*

Bring a large pot of water to a boil over high heat.

While waiting for the water to boil, place the almonds in a small skillet over medium-low heat. Toast for 7 minutes, stirring or shaking the skillet occasionally, until fragrant and slightly golden. Set aside.

When the water boils, salt it and add the bucatini. Cook according to the package directions.

Meanwhile, in a food processor, combine the toasted almonds, sun-dried tomatoes, oil, anchovies, garlic, basil, oregano, and salt and process about 1 minute, until just blended.

Reserving ½ cup of the cooking water, drain the pasta in a colander and return it to the pot.

Add the ½ cup pasta cooking water to the sauce in the food processor. Pulse a few times until combined. Add the sauce to the pasta and toss well to coat. Serve topped with the Parmesan.

NUTRITION PER SERVING: 497 calories, 64 g carbs, 5 g fiber, 16 g protein, 21 g total fat, 3 g saturated fat, 606 mg sodium

**QUICK TIP** Delicious with spaghetti, the sauce also holds up well against bucatini, a thicker, hollow pasta.

# FETTUCCINE WITH SPINACH AND FETA SAUCE

Recipe by FRANCES PRICE, R.D.

**MAKES 4 SERVINGS**
**TOTAL TIME: 25 MINUTES**

- 1½ cups crumbled feta cheese (6 ounces)
- 3 scallions, sliced
- 2 tablespoons extra-virgin olive oil
- Juice of 1 lemon
- ½ teaspoon dried dill
- ½ teaspoon ground black pepper
- 1 package (12 ounces) spinach fettuccine or linguine
- 8 ounces baby spinach

*Fresh, bright, and tangy-tasting, this dish will become a go-to recipe for quick weeknight meals. Don't be tempted to substitute a different herb for the dill—it adds a unique flavor to the dish.*

Bring a large pot of water to a boil over high heat.

While waiting for the water to boil, in a small bowl, combine the feta, scallions, oil, lemon juice, dill, and pepper and stir until well combined. Set aside.

When the water boils, salt it, then add the fettuccine and cook according to the package directions, adding the spinach during the last 30 seconds of cooking (stir the spinach into the water and push it under the water to wilt it).

Reserving ½ cup of the pasta cooking water, drain the pasta and spinach in a colander and return the pasta and spinach to the pot. Add the feta mixture and the ½ cup pasta cooking water and toss until well combined.

NUTRITION PER SERVING: 513 calories, 71 g carbs, 6 g fiber, 19 g protein, 18 g total fat, 8 g saturated fat, 651 mg sodium

QUICK TIP You can also make this using fresh fettuccine, which cooks even faster than dried.

# TUNA CAPRESE PASTA SALAD

Recipe by MATTHEW KADEY, M.S., R.D.

**MAKES 4 SERVINGS**
**TOTAL TIME: 30 MINUTES**

- 1 box (12 ounces) fusilli or penne
- 2 cans (5 ounces each) water-packed albacore tuna, drained
- 1 pint cherry tomatoes, halved
- 6 ounces bocconcini (small fresh mozzarella balls), halved
- 1 teaspoon grated lemon zest
- 1 tablespoon capers, drained
- 2 tablespoons extra-virgin olive oil
- 1 tablespoon red wine vinegar or lemon juice
- 2 cloves garlic, minced
- 2 teaspoons Italian seasoning
- ¼ teaspoon salt
- ¼ teaspoon ground black pepper
- ¼ cup chopped fresh basil

*Protein-packed tuna is rich in selenium, an antioxidant that may ease post-exercise oxidative cell damage. Look for pole- and line-caught canned tuna; it's fished in an environmentally sustainable way and is lower in mercury than conventional varieties.*

Bring a large pot of water to a boil over high heat. When the water boils, salt it and add the fusilli. Cook according to the package directions.

While the pasta cooks, in a large bowl, combine the tuna, tomatoes, bocconcini, lemon zest, and capers. Set aside.

In a small bowl, whisk together the oil, vinegar, garlic, Italian seasoning, salt, and pepper. Set aside.

Drain the penne in a colander and return it to the pot. Add the tuna mixture. Drizzle with the dressing. Toss well to combine. Serve topped with the basil.

NUTRITION PER SERVING: 573 calories, 67 g carbs, 4 g fiber, 33 g protein, 19 g total fat, 7 g saturated fat, 391 mg sodium

**QUICK TIP** Rather than slicing each cherry tomato individually, place them between two plastic lids, with the bottom lid upside down. Press down gently on the top lid and use a serrated knife to slice horizontally all the way through the tomatoes.

# ITERRANEAN CHICKEN AND PENNE

Recipe by MATTHEW KADEY, M.S., R.D.

**MAKES 6 SERVINGS**
**TOTAL TIME: 30 MINUTES**

- 1 box (12 ounces) shells, penne, or fusilli
- ¼ cup pine nuts
- 3 tablespoons extra-virgin olive oil
- 1½ tablespoons red wine vinegar
- 3 cloves garlic, minced
- 1 tablespoon Italian seasoning
- ¼ teaspoon ground black pepper
- 2 cups chopped rotisserie chicken breast
- 3 cups baby spinach
- ¾ cup quartered marinated artichoke hearts, drained
- ½ cup slivered oil-packed sun-dried tomatoes
- ¼ cup crumbled feta cheese (1 ounce)
- ¼ cup pitted and chopped olives, such as kalamata

*Quick and convenient, rotisserie chicken packs protein, B vitamins, and immune-boosting zinc, while the nitrates found in spinach may help bolster oxygen delivery to muscles.*

Bring a large pot of water to a boil over high heat. When the water boils, salt it and add the penne. Cook according to the package directions.

While the pasta cooks, heat a dry skillet over medium heat. Add the pine nuts and toast, shaking the skillet often, for 3 minutes, or until the nuts are lightly browned. Set aside.

In a small bowl, whisk together the oil, vinegar, garlic, Italian seasoning, and pepper. Set aside.

Drain the penne in a colander and return them to the pot. Add the chicken, spinach, artichoke hearts, sun-dried tomatoes, feta, and olives. Drizzle with the dressing and toss well to combine.

Serve garnished with the toasted pine nuts.

NUTRITION PER SERVING: 489 calories, 50 g carbs, 4 g fiber, 25 g protein, 22 g total fat, 3.5 g saturated fat, 680 mg sodium

# LINGUINE WITH GREEN EGGS AND TOMATOES

Recipe by MATTHEW KADEY, M.S., R.D.

**MAKES 4 SERVINGS**
**TOTAL TIME: 25 MINUTES**

- 1 box (12 ounces) linguine, spaghetti, or tagliatelle
- ½ tablespoon canola oil
- 4 large eggs
- 2 cups shredded radicchio (1 small head)
- 1 pint cherry tomatoes, halved
- ¼ cup pesto
- 1 teaspoon hot sauce

*Top your pasta with a perfectly fried egg for gooey richness and plenty of vitamin $B_{12}$, a nutrient needed to maintain nervous system functioning. The olive oil in pesto supplies oleocanthal, an anti-inflammatory compound.*

Bring a large pot of water to a boil over high heat. When the water boils, salt it and add the linguine. Cook according to the package directions.

While the pasta cooks, in a large skillet, heat the oil over medium-high heat. Crack the eggs into the skillet and cook for 2 minutes, or until the underside is firm and lightly browned. Flip the eggs over with a spatula and cook 10 seconds longer, or until they reach the desired doneness. Transfer the eggs to a plate and cover with foil or an inverted plate to keep warm.

Drain the linguine in a colander and return it to the pot. Add the radicchio, tomatoes, and pesto. Toss well to evenly coat the ingredients with the pesto.

Divide the pasta among 4 shallow bowls. Top each serving with one fried egg and ¼ teaspoon hot sauce.

NUTRITION PER SERVING: 508 calories, 69 g carbs, 4 g fiber, 21 g protein, 17 g total fat, 4 g saturated fat, 308 mg sodium

QUICK TIP To save on prep time, shred the radicchio and slice the cherry tomatoes while waiting for the water to boil.

# SPAGHETTI WITH KALE AND NAVY BEANS

Recipe by MATTHEW KADEY, M.S., R.D.

**MAKES 6 SERVINGS**
**TOTAL TIME: 30 MINUTES**

- 1 box (1 pound) spaghetti, fettuccine, or linguine
- 3 tablespoons extra-virgin olive oil
- Juice of ½ lemon
- 2 cloves garlic, minced
- ¼ teaspoon salt
- ¼ teaspoon ground black pepper
- 1 can (15 ounces) navy beans, drained and rinsed
- 6 cups baby kale (5 to 6 ounces)
- 1 cup Peppadew peppers or roasted red peppers, sliced
- ⅓ cup chopped fresh flat-leaf parsley
- ¼ cup sliced almonds
- ¼ cup grated pecorino or Parmesan cheese

*Baby kale is smart choice when you're in a hurry to get dinner on the table. It's loaded with all the same nutrients found in larger kale leaves, including vitamins A, C, and K, but it's tender enough to serve raw and comes prewashed and ready to eat. Look for it near packaged salad mixes in the produce aisle. Peppadew peppers (located in the deli bar) infuse pasta dishes with a low-calorie sweet-spicy punch.*

Bring a large pot of water to a boil over high heat. When the water boils, salt it and add the spaghetti. Cook according to the package directions.

While the pasta cooks, in a small bowl, whisk together the oil, lemon juice, garlic, salt, and pepper.

Drain the spaghetti in a colander and return it to the pot. Add the beans, kale, Peppadews, parsley, and almonds. Drizzle with the dressing and toss well to combine.

Serve sprinkled with the cheese.

NUTRITION PER SERVING: 506 calories, 82 g carbs, 8 g fiber, 18 g protein, 12 g total fat, 2 g saturated fat, 501 mg sodium

**QUICK TIP** While waiting for the water to boil, slice the Peppadew peppers and chop the parsley.

# ROTINI WITH PEARS AND PROSCIUTTO

Recipe by MATTHEW KADEY, M.S., R.D.

**MAKES 6 SERVINGS**
**TOTAL TIME: 30 MINUTES**

- 1 box (12 ounces) rotini, fusilli, or bow-tie
- 3 tablespoons extra-virgin olive oil
- 1 tablespoon apple cider vinegar
- 2 cloves garlic, minced
- ¼ teaspoon ground black pepper
- 3 ounces chopped prosciutto
- 2 pears, sliced
- 2 cups very thinly sliced fennel (about 1 medium bulb)
- 2 cups baby arugula
- ½ cup chopped walnuts
- ¼ cup crumbled blue cheese or shaved Parmesan cheese

*Salty prosciutto helps replenish lost electrolytes after a sweaty run and strikes a perfect balance with sweet, juicy pears. Look for packages of already-chopped prosciutto next to bacon in the refrigerated section at the grocery store.*

Bring a large pot of water to a boil over high heat. When the water boils, salt it and add the rotini. Cook according to the package directions.

While the pasta cooks, in a small bowl, whisk together the oil, vinegar, garlic, and pepper.

Drain the rotini in a colander and return it to the pot. Add the prosciutto, pears, fennel, arugula, and walnuts. Drizzle with the dressing. Toss well to combine.

Serve garnished with the cheese.

NUTRITION PER SERVING: 646 calories, 83 g carbs, 8 g fiber, 24 g protein, 26 g total fat, 4.5 g saturated fat, 776 mg sodium

**QUICK TIP:** To save time, slice the pears and fennel while waiting for the pasta water to come to a boil.

# BOW-TIES WITH ROASTED CHERRY TOMATOES

Recipe by MELISSA LASHER

**MAKES 4 SERVINGS**
**TOTAL TIME: 30 MINUTES**

2 pints multicolored cherry tomatoes

1 cup quartered green beans

1 tablespoon extra-virgin olive oil

¼ teaspoon salt

1 box (12 ounces) farfalle

½ pound peeled and deveined medium shrimp

⅓ cup pesto

*If you're really short on time, don't roast the tomatoes and green beans. Use frozen cut green beans, adding them to the pasta water when you add the shrimp. Omit the olive oil and salt and simply add the tomatoes to the drained pasta as directed.*

Preheat the oven to 450°F.

Bring a large pot of water to a boil over high heat.

Arrange the tomatoes and green beans on a baking sheet and drizzle with the oil. Sprinkle with the salt. Toss well to coat. Roast for 12 minutes, or until the tomatoes begin to burst. Set aside.

Meanwhile, when the water boils, salt it and add the farfalle. Cook according to the package directions. Three minutes before the pasta is done, add the shrimp (when cooked, the shrimp should be pink and opaque).

Drain the pasta and shrimp in a colander and return to the pot. Add the roasted tomatoes, green beans, and pesto. Toss well to combine.

NUTRITION PER SERVING: 519 calories, 73 g carbs, 6 g fiber, 25 g protein, 15 g total fat, 3.5 g saturated fat, 696 mg sodium

# CAVATAPPI WITH PEAS AND PROSCIUTTO

Recipe by NATE APPLEMAN

**MAKES 6 SERVINGS**
**TOTAL TIME: 25 MINUTES**

- 1 box (1 pound) cavatappi or other spiral pasta
- 1½ cups fresh spring peas
- 1 tablespoon extra-virgin olive oil
- 2 cloves garlic, minced
- ½ teaspoon ground black pepper, or more to taste
- ½ cup grated pecorino or Parmesan cheese
- Juice of ½ lemon
- 4 ounces (about 8 thin slices) prosciutto, torn into bite-size pieces

*"This is an easy pasta to whip up when short on time," says* Runner's World *contributing chef Nate Appleman. It features one of his favorite ingredients: prosciutto. Just a little bit of this flavor-packed meat adds richness while keeping calories in check.*

Bring a large pot of water to a boil. When it boils, salt it and add the cavatappi. Cook according to the package directions. Two minutes before the pasta is cooked, add the peas.

Meanwhile, in a large skillet, heat the oil over medium heat. Add the garlic and cook for 1 to 2 minutes, until slightly browned.

Reserving ¼ cup pasta cooking water, drain the pasta and peas in a colander. Add the peas, pasta, and reserved cooking water to the skillet, toss, and heat through, about 1 minute. Add the pepper, cheese, and lemon juice and toss to combine.

Serve the pasta in shallow bowls and place the prosciutto over top, letting the heat from the pasta warm the meat.

**NUTRITION PER SERVING:** 403 calories, 63 g carbs, 4 g fiber, 20 g protein, 8 g total fat, 2.5 g saturated fat, 654 mg sodium

**QUICK TIP** If you can find fresh, in-season peas, use them here. Otherwise, frozen peas will work just fine; add them 1 minute sooner in the recipe.

# COCONUT SHRIMP WITH RICE NOODLES

Recipe by MATTHEW KADEY, M.S., R.D.

**MAKES 4 SERVINGS**
**TOTAL TIME: 20 MINUTES**

- 1 package (9 ounces) rice vermicelli noodles
- 1 tablespoon canola oil
- 1 pound peeled and deveined large shrimp
- 4 cups (8 to 9 ounces) broccoli florets
- 1 red bell pepper, sliced
- 1 can (14 ounces) light coconut milk
- 2 tablespoons yellow curry paste
- Juice of 1 lime
- ¼ cup chopped unsalted peanuts
- ¼ cup chopped fresh cilantro

*Shrimp are a source of heart-healthy omega-3 fats and vitamin D, a nutrient shown to help reduce inflammation following a workout. Quick-cooking rice noodles, which require just a quick soak, are a great choice when you're short on time.*

Soak the noodles in a large bowl of hot tap water for 5 minutes, or until softened. Drain the noodles in a colander and then rinse them under cool water. Set aside.

Meanwhile, in a wok or large, deep pot, heat ½ tablespoon of the oil over medium-high heat. Add the shrimp and cook for 3 to 5 minutes, or until pink and opaque. Remove from the wok and set aside.

Add the remaining ½ tablespoon oil to the wok, along with the broccoli and bell pepper. Cook for 3 to 5 minutes, or until the vegetables are slightly softened. Remove from the wok and set aside with the shrimp.

Increase the heat under the wok to high and add the coconut milk, curry paste, and lime juice. Stir until heated through and well combined. Return the shrimp, vegetables, and noodles to the wok. Toss well to coat with the sauce.

Serve garnished with the peanuts and cilantro.

**NUTRITION PER SERVING:** 517 calories, 66 g carbs, 5 g fiber, 25 g protein, 16 g total fat, 5 g saturated fat, 981 mg sodium

**QUICK TIP** Yellow curry paste is available at many supermarkets and Asian markets and some specialty grocers. It's milder than green or red curry paste, but either may be substituted.

# SPAGHETTI CARBONARA

Recipe by JOANNA SAYAGO GOLUB

**MAKES 6 SERVINGS**
**TOTAL TIME: 30 MINUTES**

- 6 slices bacon, chopped
- 1 box (1 pound) spaghetti
- ½ sweet onion, chopped
- 3 large eggs
- ¼ teaspoon salt
- ½ teaspoon ground black pepper, plus more to taste
- 1 cup frozen peas
- ¾ cup grated Parmesan cheese
- 2 tablespoons chopped fresh flat-leaf parsley

*This classic Italian pasta is as satisfyingly delicious as it is easy to make. While not traditional, sautéed onions add a note of sweetness, and peas provide a pop of color and nutrients.*

Bring a large pot of water to a boil over high heat.

While waiting for the water to boil, heat a large skillet over medium-high heat. Add the bacon and cook, stirring occasionally, for 5 minutes, or until the bacon is browned and crisp. Using a slotted spoon, remove the bacon to a plate lined with a paper towel. Set aside.

Meanwhile, when the water boils, salt it and add the spaghetti. Cook according to the package directions.

Meanwhile, return the skillet to the stove over medium heat (if there is more than 1 tablespoon of bacon fat in the skillet, drain it first). Add the onion and cook, stirring occasionally, for 4 minutes, or until the onion is softened and translucent. Set aside.

In a bowl, beat the eggs well with a fork. Season with the salt and pepper.

Two minutes before the spaghetti is done, add the peas. Reserving ½ cup of the cooking water, drain the spaghetti and peas in a colander and return to the still-hot pot. Immediately add the eggs, reserved ½ cup cooking water, and the onions. Toss well to coat the spaghetti (the residual heat from the pasta will gently cook the eggs as they coat the spaghetti). Sprinkle with the Parmesan, bacon, and parsley, and toss well again.

Serve with additional ground black pepper, if desired.

**NUTRITION PER SERVING:** 443 calories, 61 g carbs, 4 g fiber, 21 g protein, 12 g total fat, 4.5 g saturated fat, 494 mg sodium

# SPAGHETTI WITH TUNA SAUCE

**Recipe by PAM ANDERSON**

**MAKES 6 SERVINGS**
**TOTAL TIME: 30 MINUTES**

- 2 tablespoons extra-virgin olive oil
- 3 cloves garlic, minced
- ½ teaspoon red pepper flakes
- 1 can (28 ounces) crushed tomatoes
- 2 cans (5 ounces each) albacore tuna, not drained
- ½ cup pitted and chopped kalamata or oil-cured olives
- Pinch of dried oregano
- 1 box (1 pound) spaghetti
- ¼ cup grated Parmesan cheese

*Tuna is a lean source of protein, packing 20 grams into just 3 ounces of fish.* Runner's World *contributing chef Pam Anderson prefers pole- and line-caught tuna because it is environmentally sustainable. And compared with mass-fished tuna, pole- and line-caught fish are lower in mercury and higher in omega-3 fatty acids. "Typically fish and cheese don't mix," says Anderson, "but I like a sprinkling of Parmesan over this bold sauce."*

Bring a large pot of water to a boil over high heat.

While waiting for the water to boil, heat a second large pot over medium-high heat. Add the oil, garlic, and pepper flakes. Cook for 2 minutes, or until the garlic turns golden. Stir in the tomatoes, tuna, olives, and oregano. Simmer, partially covered, for 10 minutes.

Meanwhile, when the water boils, salt it and add the spaghetti. Cook according to the package directions. Drain the spaghetti in a colander and add it to the pot with the sauce. Toss well to coat. Sprinkle with the Parmesan and toss well again.

NUTRITION PER SERVING: 476 calories, 68 g carbs, 5 g fiber, 25 g protein, 12 g total fat, 2 g saturated fat, 640 mg sodium

# PENNE WITH BROCCOLI RABE AND SAUSAGE

**Recipe by THE RODALE TEST KITCHEN**

**MAKES 6 SERVINGS**
**TOTAL TIME: 30 MINUTES**

- 1 bunch (about 1 pound) broccoli rabe, trimmed and roughly chopped
- 1 box (12 to 13.25 ounces) multigrain penne
- 1½ tablespoons extra-virgin olive oil
- ¾ pound bulk sweet Italian sausage
- 6 cloves garlic, sliced
- ½ teaspoon red pepper flakes (optional)
- 1 cup low-sodium chicken broth
- ½ teaspoon salt
- ¼ cup grated Parmesan cheese

*You don't need a lot of sausage to add lots to flavor—and protein—to your meals. Here, just 2 ounces per serving packs more than 20 grams of protein. "Bulk" sausage is simply ground sausage that hasn't been put in casings. Look for it at the meat counter.*

Bring a large pot of water to a boil over high heat. When the water boils, lightly salt it. Add the broccoli rabe and cook for 2 minutes, or until bright-green and crisp-tender. With kitchen tongs or a slotted spoon, transfer the broccoli rabe to a colander and rinse under very cold water. Drain well and gently squeeze to remove any excess water. Set aside.

Return the water in the pot to a boil. Add the penne and cook according to package directions.

Meanwhile, heat the oil in a large skillet over medium-high heat. Add the sausage and cook, stirring and breaking it into smaller pieces with a wooden spoon, for 4 to 6 minutes, until no longer pink. Add the garlic and red pepper flakes (if using) and cook for 1 to 2 minutes or until lightly golden. Pour in the broth, increase the heat to high, and bring to a boil. Cook for 3 to 4 minutes, or until the broth is reduced by about half. Stir in the broccoli rabe and salt. Cook, stirring often, for 1 to 2 minutes, or until hot.

When the penne is cooked, drain it in a colander. Return the pasta to the pot. Add the sausage mixture and Parmesan and toss well to coat.

**NUTRITION PER SERVING:** 400 calories, 53 g carbs, 6 g fiber, 22 g protein, 11 g total fat, 3 g saturated fat, 650 mg sodium

**QUICK TIP** You can also make this with link sausage—just remove the casings before cooking (crumbling the meat helps distribute it evenly through the dish).

# BOLOGNESE OVER SHELLS

Recipe by THE RODALE TEST KITCHEN

**MAKES 4 SERVINGS**
**TOTAL TIME: 30 MINUTES**

- 1 box (12 ounces) whole wheat shells or penne
- ¼ cup extra-virgin olive oil
- ½ pound extra-lean (95%) ground beef
- 1 teaspoon dried basil
- 1 onion, chopped
- 1 carrot, finely chopped
- 3 cloves garlic, minced
- 1 can (28 ounces) fire-roasted diced tomatoes
- 3 tablespoons tomato paste
- ¼ teaspoon salt
- ⅓ cup grated Parmesan cheese (plus more for serving, optional)
- ¼ teaspoon ground black pepper

*This Bolognese is proof that a good meat sauce does not have to simmer for hours on end. Fire-roasted tomatoes and tomato paste give it extra depth with just 10 minutes of simmering. Hearty, whole wheat pasta is a good match for the meaty sauce.*

Bring a large pot of water to a boil over high heat. When the water boils, salt it and add the shells. Cook according to the package directions. Drain the shells in a colander and set aside.

Meanwhile, in a large skillet, heat the oil over medium-high heat. Add the beef and basil and cook, breaking the beef into smaller pieces with a wooden spoon, for 4 to 5 minutes, until starting to brown.

Stir in the onion, carrot, and garlic and cook for 3 to 4 minutes, or until the beef is browned and the vegetables are slightly softened.

Add the tomatoes (with their juices), tomato paste, and salt and stir until well combined. Increase the heat to high and bring to a boil. Reduce the heat to medium and simmer for 10 minutes.

Add the penne to the sauce and toss to combine. Sprinkle in the Parmesan and pepper, and toss well again. Serve with additional Parmesan, if desired.

NUTRITION PER SERVING: 593 calories, 81 g carb, 10 g fiber, 29 g protein, 19 g total fat, 4 g saturated fat, 897 mg sodium

# 7

# VEGETARIAN MAINS and SIDES

## Mains

## Sides

# PIZZA MARGHERITA WITH MAKE-AHEAD TOMATO SAUCE

Recipe by MATTHEW KADEY, M.S., R.D.

**MAKES 4 SERVINGS**
**TOTAL TIME: 20 MINUTES**

- 1 pound store-bought pizza dough
- 1 teaspoon plus 1 tablespoon extra-virgin olive oil
- 1 cup Make-Ahead Tomato Sauce (page 156), or any jarred tomato sauce
- 4 ounces fresh mozzarella cheese, patted dry and torn into ¾-inch pieces
- 6 large basil leaves, roughly torn
- ¼ cup grated or shaved Parmesan cheese
- ½ teaspoon ground black pepper

*Pizza doesn't get simpler or more delicious than this. Fresh mozzarella melts beautifully and, thanks to its high water content, is naturally lower in fat than many hard cheeses.*

Preheat the oven to 500°F. Lightly coat a baking sheet with cooking spray.

Roll the dough into a 12 x 9-inch rectangle no more than ¼ inch thick. Brush 1 teaspoon of the oil over a 1-inch border all around the rectangle.

Spread the tomato sauce over the dough, leaving the 1-inch border uncovered. Lay the mozzarella pieces on the sauce. Bake for 10 minutes, or until the crust is golden and crisp and the cheese is bubbling. Top with the basil. Drizzle with the remaining 1 tablespoon oil. Sprinkle with the Parmesan and pepper.

NUTRITION PER SERVING: 387 calories, 49 g carbs, 2 g fiber, 14 g protein, 17 g total fat, 5 g saturated fat, 473 mg sodium

QUICK TIP If you don't want to make tomato sauce and don't have any on hand, substitute 2 fresh plum tomatoes, sliced crosswise.

# MAKE-AHEAD TOMATO SAUCE

Recipe by MATTHEW KADEY, M.S., R.D.

**MAKES 3 CUPS**
**TOTAL TIME: 30 MINUTES**

2 tablespoons extra-virgin olive oil

3 cloves garlic, minced

1 can (28 ounces) crushed tomatoes

2 tablespoons tomato paste

2 tablespoons red wine vinegar

1 teaspoon dried basil

1 teaspoon dried oregano

½ teaspoon salt

½ teaspoon red pepper flakes

*Make a batch of this tomato sauce and store it in ½-cup portions in the freezer so you can add it to the Pizza Margherita (page 154), or any home-made pizza, whenever you need it. Cooking the sauce in a sauté pan (or straight-sided skillet) helps reduce splattering, but you can also cook it in a traditional skillet instead.*

In a large sauté pan or straight-sided skillet, heat the oil over medium-high heat. Add the garlic and cook for 1 minute, or until it becomes fragrant and turns lightly golden. Add the tomatoes, tomato paste, vinegar, basil, oregano, salt, and pepper flakes. Stir to combine. Bring to a boil, then reduce the heat to low and simmer, uncovered and stirring occasionally, for 20 minutes, or until slightly thickened.

Let the sauce cool, then divide into ½-cup portions and freeze. When ready to use, defrost in the microwave until heated through.

NUTRITION PER ½-CUP SERVING: 93 calories, 11 g carbs, 3 g fiber, 3 g protein, 5 g total fat, 0.5 g saturated fat, 412 mg sodium

# SMOKY SQUASH FLATBREAD WITH BALSAMIC GLAZE

Recipe by MATTHEW KADEY, M.S., R.D., AND THE RODALE TEST KITCHEN

**MAKES 4 SERVINGS**
**TOTAL TIME: 25 MINUTES**

## Sauce

- 1 package (10 or 12 ounces) frozen winter squash puree, thawed
- ½ cup grated Parmesan or pecorino cheese
- 2 cloves garlic, minced
- ¾ teaspoon smoked paprika
- ½ teaspoon ground cumin
- ¼ teaspoon ground nutmeg
- ¼ teaspoon salt
- ¼ teaspoon ground black pepper

## Flatbreads and Glaze

- ¼ pound Brussels sprouts, stems trimmed
- 1 tablespoon extra-virgin olive oil
- 4 whole wheat naan flatbreads
- ¼ cup crumbled goat cheese (1 ounce)
- ¼ cup chopped hazelnuts (1 ounce)
- ⅓ cup balsamic vinegar
- 2 teaspoons light brown sugar

*Made with frozen winter squash puree, the sauce for these flatbreads comes together in no time. Look for the squash puree in the freezer aisle and stock up on a few packages so you have them on hand when needed. Hazelnuts add heart-healthy fats and a satisfying crunch.*

Preheat the oven to 400°F. Line 2 baking sheets with parchment paper or foil.

Make the sauce: In a small bowl, combine the squash, Parmesan, garlic, smoked paprika, cumin, nutmeg, salt, and pepper. Stir until well combined. Set aside.

For the flatbreads: In a food processor fitted with a shredding disk, shred the Brussels sprouts. (Alternatively, trim and halve them, then thinly slice with a sharp knife.) In a bowl, toss the shredded sprouts with the olive oil.

Set the flatbreads on the lined baking sheets. Spread an even amount of the squash sauce over them, leaving a ½-inch border uncovered. Top with the Brussels sprouts, goat cheese, and hazelnuts. Bake for 10 minutes, or until the crust is golden brown and the cheese begins to melt.

Meanwhile, for the glaze: In a small saucepan, combine the vinegar and brown sugar and bring to a simmer over medium heat. Cook for 6 minutes, or until syrupy and reduced to 2 tablespoons.

Serve the flatbreads drizzled with the balsamic glaze.

NUTRITION PER SERVING: 585 calories, 75 g carbs, 10 g fiber, 19 g protein, 24 g total fat, 6 g saturated fat, 960 mg sodium

**QUICK TIP** Don't have time to make a balsamic glaze? Pick up a bottled version at the supermarket.

# CHICKPEA CHERRY FRITTATA

Recipe by SAM TALBOT

**MAKES 4 SERVINGS**
**TOTAL TIME: 30 MINUTES**

- 8 large eggs
- 1 can (15 ounces) chickpeas, drained and rinsed
- 1 cup chopped fresh cherries or ½ cup chopped dried cherries
- 1 cup crumbled goat cheese (4 ounces)
- ¼ cup unsweetened almond milk or dairy milk
- 1 tablespoon chopped fresh thyme leaves
- 2 tablespoons agave syrup or honey
- 1 teaspoon cream of tartar
- 1 tablespoon extra-virgin olive oil
- ¼ cup loosely packed torn fresh mint leaves

*Chickpeas, cherries, and eggs might seem like an unusual combination, but "they make a bold-flavored dish," says runner, surfer, and chef Sam Talbot, author of* The Sweet Life. *The frittata is rich in protein (thanks to the chickpeas and eggs) and inflammation-reducing antioxidants (from the cherries). Talbot, who was diagnosed with diabetes as a child, uses agave syrup in this recipe because it is low on the glycemic index. But you can substitute an equal amount of honey as an alternative.*

Preheat the oven to 350°F.

In a large bowl, lightly whisk the eggs. Stir in the chickpeas, cherries, goat cheese, almond milk, thyme, agave syrup, and cream of tartar.

In a medium ovenproof skillet, heat the oil over medium heat. Pour the egg mixture into the skillet and cook for 2 minutes without stirring.

Transfer the skillet to the oven and bake for 15 to 20 minutes, until the eggs are puffed and set in the middle. Let the frittata cool briefly.

With a silicone spatula, gently work the frittata out of the pan and transfer it to a cutting board. Cut the frittata into wedges and serve garnished with the mint.

NUTRITION PER SERVING: 398 calories, 26 g carbs, 4 g fiber, 23 g protein, 23 g total fat, 9.5 g saturated fat, 380 mg sodium

# COUSCOUS WITH WHITE BEANS AND ROASTED RED PEPPER

**Recipe by THE RODALE TEST KITCHEN**

**MAKES 6 SERVINGS**
**TOTAL TIME: 30 MINUTES**

*Quick-cooking and high in carbs, whole wheat couscous is an ideal energy source for runners short on time. It makes a great base for this easily customized dish.*

2 cups water

1½ cups whole wheat couscous

1 carrot, quartered lengthwise and thinly sliced crosswise

¾ teaspoon salt

¼ teaspoon ground black pepper

¼ cup extra-virgin olive oil

⅓ cup fresh lemon juice (about 2 lemons)

1 can (15 ounces) Great Northern beans, or other large white bean, drained and rinsed

⅓ cup pine nuts

1 cup marinated roasted red peppers, cut into 1-inch pieces

1 cup fresh mint leaves, torn

1 cup crumbled feta cheese (4 ounces)

In a medium saucepan, bring the water to a boil. Add the couscous, carrot, salt, and pepper and remove from the heat. Cover and let stand for 5 minutes, or until the water has been absorbed.

With a fork, gently stir in the oil and lemon juice. Add the beans and fluff with the fork. Let cool slightly.

Meanwhile, in a small skillet over medium heat, toast the pine nuts, gently shaking the skillet occasionally, for 3 to 5 minutes, until fragrant and starting to turn brown. Transfer to the couscous.

With a fork, fold in the roasted peppers, mint, and feta. Serve warm, at room temperature, or chilled.

NUTRITION PER SERVING: 411 calories, 51 g carbs, 10 g fiber, 14 g protein, 19 g fat, 5 g saturated fat, 586 mg sodium

**QUICK TIP** You can use any light-colored beans, like chickpeas, in place of the Great Northern beans. Try sliced sun-dried tomatoes instead of the roasted red pepper. And feel free to substitute a different fresh herb, such as parsley or basil.

# GRILLED EGGPLANT AND FRESH MOZZARELLA SANDWICHES

Recipe by THE RODALE TEST KITCHEN

**MAKES 4 SERVINGS**
**TOTAL TIME: 25 MINUTES**

Canola oil, for the grill

2 eggplants (1¼ pounds each), cut lengthwise into 12 (⅓-inch-thick) slices

2 tablespoons extra-virgin olive oil

½ teaspoon salt

¼ teaspoon ground black pepper

2 medium tomatoes, sliced

12 large fresh basil leaves

8 slices (¼-inch) fresh mozzarella cheese (4 ounces)

4 large ciabatta rolls, split

2 tablespoons balsamic vinegar

*This sandwich proves that a meal doesn't have to be complicated to be delicious. Ripe summer tomatoes are a rich source of vitamin C and lycopene, while low-calorie eggplant provides antioxidants with heart-protective qualities. If you like, top the sandwich with pesto or spread on Edamame-Basil Dip (page 58) for extra flavor.*

Brush a grill rack with canola oil and heat the grill to medium-high heat.

Brush both sides of the eggplant slices lightly with the olive oil and season with the salt and pepper. Place the eggplant over direct heat. Grill for 5 to 7 minutes per side, until grill marks form and the eggplant is lightly browned and tender.

To assemble the sandwiches, layer 3 eggplant slices, 2 tomato slices, 3 basil leaves, and 2 mozzarella slices on the bottom half of each ciabatta roll. Drizzle with the balsamic vinegar. Cover with the tops of the rolls and serve.

NUTRITION PER SERVING: 384 calories, 50 g carbs, 8 g fiber, 12 g protein, 15 g total fat, 5 g saturated fat, 665 mg sodium

QUICK TIP Anytime you're firing up the grill for dinner, throw some extra vegetables on to cook. You can add the leftovers to pasta, salads, and other sandwiches for quick meals throughout the week.

# ASPARAGUS AND MUSHROOM RICE BOWL

Recipe by MATTHEW KADEY, M.S., R.D.

**MAKES 4 SERVINGS**
**TOTAL TIME: 20 MINUTES**

*Just ½ cup of cooked, chopped asparagus packs 57 percent of your daily need for vitamin K, which plays a role in promoting bone and heart health. Mushrooms provide B vitamins, copper, and the antioxidant mineral selenium—while also adding a meaty quality and savory flavor to the dish.*

### Rice Bowl

- 2 cups 10-minute brown rice
- 1 tablespoon plus 1 teaspoon extra-virgin olive oil
- 1 pound asparagus, trimmed and cut into 1-inch pieces
- 1 package (8 ounces) sliced cremini mushrooms
- 4 large eggs

### Dressing and Garnish

- 3 tablespoons extra-virgin olive oil
- Juice of ½ lemon
- 2 tablespoons finely chopped fresh dill
- 1 clove garlic, minced
- ½ teaspoon salt
- ¼ teaspoon red pepper flakes
- ¼ teaspoon ground black pepper
- 1 tablespoon grated Parmesan (optional)

Make the rice bowl: Cook the rice according to the package directions.

Meanwhile, in a large skillet, heat 1 tablespoon of the oil over medium heat. Add the asparagus and mushrooms and cook for 5 minutes, or until the mushrooms have softened and darkened and the asparagus is just tender. Transfer to a bowl and set aside.

Return the skillet to the heat and add the remaining 1 teaspoon oil. Add the eggs and cook for 3 minutes. Flip the eggs and cook 30 seconds more, or until they reach desired doneness. Transfer to a plate and cover with foil to keep warm.

Make the dressing: In a small bowl, whisk together the oil, lemon juice, dill, garlic, salt, pepper flakes, and black pepper.

Divide the rice among 4 bowls. Top each with a portion of the vegetables and 1 egg. Drizzle with the dressing. If desired, sprinkle with the Parmesan.

NUTRITION PER SERVING: 387 calories, 39 g carbs, 4 g fiber, 13 g protein, 21 g total fat, 3.5 g saturated fat, 373 mg sodium

> **QUICK TIP** Made from parboiled whole grain brown rice, 10-minute brown rice is a quick alternative to traditional brown rice, which can take 30 to 40 minutes to cook.

# SWEET POTATO-BLACK BEAN FALAFEL

### Recipe by MATTHEW KADEY, M.S., R.D.

**MAKES 4 SERVINGS**
**TOTAL TIME: 30 MINUTES**

### Falafel

- 2 medium sweet potatoes (about 1 pound total)
- 1 can (15 ounces) black beans, drained and rinsed
- ⅔ cup toasted wheat germ
- ½ cup chopped red onion
- ½ cup chopped walnuts
- 1 tablespoon Dijon mustard
- 1 teaspoon ground cumin
- ¼ teaspoon salt
- ¼ teaspoon ground black pepper
- 2 tablespoons extra-virgin olive oil

### Tahini Sauce

- 2 tablespoons tahini
- 2 tablespoons water
- 2 teaspoons fresh lemon juice
- 4 large whole wheat pitas (6 to 8 inches)

*This new take on falafel combines sweet potatoes and black beans instead of using more traditional chickpeas. The resulting patties are packed with flavor, as well as carbs, protein, beta-carotene, and fiber. If you have a little extra time, instead of microwaving the potatoes, you can peel and chop them and then steam or boil in water until tender (about 5 minutes). Along with the falafel and tahini sauce, stuff the pitas with your favorite toppings, including cucumber slices, lettuce, tomato, and red onion.*

For the falafel: Prick the sweet potatoes with a fork, then set on a paper towel and microwave on high for 6 minutes, or until tender.

When cool enough to handle, halve the sweet potatoes and scoop the flesh into a bowl. Add the beans and mash together with a fork. Mix in the wheat germ, onion, walnuts, mustard, cumin, salt, and pepper until well combined.

Heat a large skillet over medium heat and add 1 tablespoon of the oil. Use a tablespoon to shape the sweet potato mixture into 16 patties (each about 2 inches long and 1 inch wide) and set the falafel patties on a plate. Add half of the falafel to the hot skillet and cook for 2 to 3 minutes per side, or until they form a crispy, golden crust. Transfer to a plate lined with paper towels. Repeat with remaining 1 tablespoon oil and falafel patties.

Make the tahini sauce: In a small bowl, stir together the tahini, water, and lemon juice.

With the tip of a knife, cut an opening in one side of each pita. Divide the falafel among the pitas and drizzle with the tahini sauce.

NUTRITION PER SERVING: 595 calories, 80 g carbs, 17 g fiber, 21 g protein, 24 g total fat, 3 g saturated fat, 822 mg sodium

# SPICED CHICKPEAS WITH SPINACH

Recipe by THE RODALE TEST KITCHEN

**MAKES 4 SERVINGS**
**TOTAL TIME: 20 MINUTES**

- 3 tablespoons plus 2 teaspoons extra-virgin olive oil
- 4 cloves garlic, thinly sliced
- 1 tablespoon paprika
- 1 teaspoon ground cumin
- ¼ teaspoon salt
- ⅛ teaspoon ground black pepper
- 1 cup soft whole grain breadcrumbs
- 1 can (15 ounces) chickpeas, drained and rinsed
- ¾ cup water
- 1 tablespoon white wine vinegar
- 5 ounces baby spinach
- 4 large eggs

*Torn pieces of bread thicken and add an earthy note to this comforting dish. If you'd like to serve it as a side, omit the fried egg. To make the fresh breadcrumbs called for in this recipe, loosely tear 2 slices of bread and put them in a food processor. Pulse until reduced to loose crumbs, about 1 minute.*

In a medium saucepan, heat 3 tablespoons of the oil over medium heat. Add the garlic and cook for 30 seconds, stirring constantly, until the garlic is translucent and fragrant. Stir in the paprika, cumin, salt, and pepper. Add the breadcrumbs and cook for 2 minutes, or until toasted.

Add the chickpeas, water, and vinegar and simmer for 3 minutes. Stir, breaking up the bread to help it dissolve into the sauce. Add the spinach and simmer, stirring occasionally, for 2 minutes, or until wilted. Keep warm.

Meanwhile, in a large skillet, heat the remaining 2 teaspoons oil over medium heat. Add the eggs and cook for 3 minutes. Flip the eggs and cook 30 seconds more, or until desired doneness.

Portion the chickpea mixture out into 4 shallow bowls. Top each with a fried egg.

NUTRITION PER SERVING: 310 calories, 21 g carbs, 7 g fiber, 13 g protein, 20 g fat, 3.5 g saturated fat, 494 mg sodium

# CHEESY POLENTA WITH CARAMELIZED MUSHROOMS

**Recipe by JENNIFER KUSHNIER**

**MAKES 4 SERVINGS**
**TOTAL TIME: 20 MINUTES**

- 1 tablespoon extra-virgin olive oil
- 1 tablespoon butter
- 1 pound assorted sliced mushrooms (such as white, cremini, and shiitake)
- 1 clove garlic, minced
- ½ teaspoon salt
- 4 cups low-sodium vegetable broth
- 1 cup quick-cooking (instant) polenta
- 4 ounces Gruyère cheese, grated (1 cup)
- 1 tablespoon chopped fresh chives or thyme

*While traditional polenta requires 30 minutes of constant stirring, quick-cooking (or "instant") versions take just a few minutes from start to finish and produce creamy, irresistible results. Look for it in boxes near specialty Italian products in the supermarket. Don't mistakenly buy precooked polenta, which is often sold in tube-shaped packages.*

In a large skillet, heat the oil and butter over medium heat until the butter is melted. Add the mushrooms and cook for 4 minutes, undisturbed, until their juices have released and their undersides begin to brown. Stir the mushrooms, then allow to cook, undisturbed, for another 4 minutes, or until a rich golden color develops and the liquid evaporates. Once the mushrooms are browned, add the garlic and ¼ teaspoon of the salt and stir until fragrant, about 1 minute. Set aside.

Meanwhile, in a medium saucepan, bring the vegetable broth to a boil over high heat. Reduce the heat to medium-low, whisk in the polenta, and cook for 3 to 4 minutes, until thickened. Add the cheese and remaining ¼ teaspoon salt and stir until incorporated.

Divide the polenta among 4 plates and spoon the mushrooms on top. Sprinkle with the chives or thyme.

**NUTRITION PER SERVING:** 419 calories, 55 g carbs, 4 g fiber, 16 g protein, 16 g total fat, 7.5 g saturated fat, 557 mg sodium

**QUICK TIP** The key to deliciously caramelized mushrooms is to leave them alone: The more you stir them, the more they'll steam instead of brown.

# TOFU PEANUT STIR-FRY

Recipe by THE RODALE TEST KITCHEN

**MAKES 4 SERVINGS**
**TOTAL TIME: 30 MINUTES**

- 1½ cups 10-minute brown rice
- 4 teaspoons canola oil
- 1 package (14 ounces) extra-firm tofu, drained, pressed (see Quick Tip), and cut into ½-inch pieces
- 1 onion, chopped
- 1 package (8 ounces) sliced mushrooms
- 3 cloves garlic, minced
- 1 tablespoon grated fresh ginger
- ½ cup frozen peas
- ½ cup salted dry-roasted peanuts
- ⅓ cup hoisin sauce
- 1 tablespoon seasoned rice vinegar
- 3 scallions, chopped

*Hoisin sauce and seasoned rice vinegar add loads of flavor to this dish. Look for both condiments in the Asian aisle in most grocery stores and keep your pantry stocked with a bottle of each for quick dinners like this one.*

Cook the rice according to the package directions.

In a large skillet, heat 2 teaspoons of the oil over medium-high heat. Add the tofu and cook for 8 to 10 minutes, turning occasionally, until lightly browned. Transfer to a plate and set aside.

Return the skillet to the stove and heat the remaining 2 teaspoons oil. Stir in the onion and cook for 1 minute. Add the mushrooms and cook for 5 to 6 minutes, stirring occasionally, until lightly browned. Stir in the garlic and ginger and cook for 30 seconds, until fragrant. Add the peas and peanuts and cook for 1 minute, until the peas are bright green. Return the tofu to the pan and add the hoisin and vinegar. Cook, stirring, for 1 minute, or until hot.

Remove from the heat and stir in the scallions. Serve over the rice.

NUTRITION PER SERVING: 595 calories, 79 g carbs, 9 g fiber, 24 g protein, 22 g total fat, 2.5 g saturated fat, 544 mg sodium

QUICK TIP Before adding the tofu to the stir-fry, press it to remove excess moisture (doing so will help the tofu hold its shape): Cut the tofu into slices, then lay the slices on a baking sheet or cutting board lined with paper towels. Cover with more paper towels and press with your hands. Cut the tofu into ½-inch pieces.

# LOADED BRUSCHETTA

Recipe by JOANNA SAYAGO GOLUB

**MAKES 4 SERVINGS**
**TOTAL TIME: 30 MINUTES**

- 8 slices (½-inch-thick) crusty Italian bread
- 3 tablespoons extra-virgin olive oil (plus more for drizzling, optional)
- 2 cloves garlic, 1 halved and 1 minced
- 3 large plum tomatoes, chopped
- 1 avocado, diced
- ¼ red onion, chopped
- 2 tablespoons chopped fresh basil
- Juice of ½ lemon
- ½ teaspoon salt
- 1 cup canned cannellini beans, drained, rinsed, and mashed with a fork
- ¼ teaspoon ground black pepper

*Topped with beans, tomatoes, and avocado, this bruschetta is hearty enough to eat as a main meal. The beans provide protein and fiber, which fill you up, while the avocado packs heart-healthy fat to keep you satisfied. You can also toast the bread in batches in a toaster rather than in the oven.*

Preheat the oven to 400°F.

Arrange the slices of bread on a baking sheet. Brush both sides with 2 tablespoons of the oil. Bake for 10 minutes, or until the edges turn golden in color. Remove from the oven and let cool for 1 minute. Rub the toasts with the cut garlic half (then discard the cut garlic). Set the toasts aside.

Meanwhile, in a bowl, combine the tomatoes, avocado, onion, basil, lemon juice, and salt. Stir well and set aside.

In a small skillet, heat the remaining 1 tablespoon oil over medium heat. Add the minced garlic and cook for 30 seconds, or until golden. Add the beans and pepper and cook, stirring often, for 3 minutes, or until the beans absorb the oil and are heated through.

Spread the mashed beans on the toasts. Top with the tomato mixture. Finish with a drizzle of olive oil, if desired.

NUTRITION PER SERVING: 344 calories, 39 g carbs, 7 g fiber, 9 g protein, 17 g total fat, 3 g saturated fat, 689 mg sodium

# SAUTÉED BABY KALE AND PINE NUTS

**Recipe by THE RODALE TEST KITCHEN**

**MAKES 4 SERVINGS**
**TOTAL TIME: 10 MINUTES**

2 tablespoons extra-virgin olive oil

2 large cloves garlic, smashed and peeled

½ teaspoon red pepper flakes

¼ cup pine nuts

16 ounces baby kale leaves

2 tablespoons water

¼ teaspoon salt

*Lightly sautéed greens make for a quick, delicious side dish any night of the week. This garlicky version gets a little kick from red pepper flakes.*

In a large, deep skillet or pot, heat the oil over medium heat. Add the garlic and pepper flakes and cook for 1 to 2 minutes, until the garlic is golden.

Discard the garlic. Add the pine nuts to the oil and cook, stirring constantly, for 1 to 2 minutes, until lightly toasted.

Add the kale, water, and salt. Cover and cook over high heat, tossing with a fork once or twice, for 4 to 5 minutes, just until wilted and tender.

NUTRITION PER SERVING: 167 calories, 8 g carbs, 3 g fiber, 4 g protein, 13 g total fat, 1 g saturated fat, 259 mg sodium

QUICK TIP If you can't find baby kale, substitute baby spinach and reduce the cooking time to 1 to 2 minutes.

# BASIL-MINT SUGAR SNAPS

**Recipe by THE RODALE TEST KITCHEN**

**MAKES 4 SERVINGS**
**TOTAL TIME: 20 MINUTES**

1½ pounds sugar snap peas, strings removed

¼ cup chopped fresh mint

¼ cup chopped fresh basil

1 tablespoon extra-virgin olive oil

1 tablespoon fresh lime juice

¾ teaspoon salt

*Mint, basil, and lime juice give these crisp-tender beans a bright, refreshing flavor. You can also make this with all basil if you prefer.*

In a steamer, cook the peas for 5 to 10 minutes, until crisp-tender.

Transfer the peas to a large bowl and add the mint, basil, oil, lime juice, and salt. Toss to combine.

NUTRITION PER SERVING: 104 calories, 13 g carbs, 5 g fiber, 5 g protein, 4 g total fat, 0.5 g saturated fat, 444 mg sodium

# ROASTED CURRY CAULIFLOWER

Recipe by JOANNA SAYAGO GOLUB

**MAKES 4 SERVINGS**
**TOTAL TIME: 25 MINUTES**

- 1 head cauliflower (2½ to 3 pounds), cored and cut into bite-size florets
- 1 tablespoon extra-virgin olive oil
- 1 teaspoon curry powder
- ½ teaspoon salt
- ¼ teaspoon ground black pepper

*As a member of the cruciferous vegetable family, cauliflower contains compounds that may inhibit cancer cell growth. Roasting it with a sprinkle of curry powder adds a golden hue and anti-inflammatory compounds.*

Preheat the oven to 450°F.

Spread the florets on a baking sheet. Drizzle with the oil. Sprinkle with the curry powder, salt, and pepper. Toss well to coat. Roast for 15 to 20 minutes, until the cauliflower is tender and browned.

NUTRITION PER SERVING: 66 calories, 7 g carbs, 3 g fiber, 3 g protein, 4 g total fat, 1 g saturated fat, 332 mg sodium

# BROCCOLI WITH LEMON-GARLIC SAUCE

Recipe by THE RODALE TEST KITCHEN

**MAKES 4 SERVINGS**
**TOTAL TIME: 20 MINUTES**

- 1 pound broccoli florets (about 8 cups)
- 1 tablespoon extra-virgin olive oil
- 1 large shallot, finely chopped
- 5 cloves garlic, minced
- 1 tablespoon butter or extra-virgin olive oil
- 2 teaspoons grated lemon zest
- 1 tablespoon fresh lemon juice
- ½ teaspoon salt
- ¼ teaspoon ground black pepper

*Just a small amount of butter adds rich flavor to this lemon-garlic sauce, but vegan runners can simply use an additional 1 tablespoon olive oil instead.*

In a steamer, cook the broccoli florets for 3 to 5 minutes, or until crisp-tender.

In a large skillet, heat the oil over medium-high heat. Add the shallot and garlic and cook for 3 to 5 minutes, until the shallot begins to brown.

Remove the skillet from the heat and stir in the butter, lemon zest, lemon juice, salt, and pepper. Stir to melt the butter.

Add the broccoli to the skillet and toss to coat with the sauce.

NUTRITION PER SERVING: 110 calories, 11 g carbs, 4 g fiber, 4 g protein, 7 g total fat, 2 g saturated fat, 348 mg sodium

**QUICK TIP** Buying cleaned and trimmed broccoli florets, rather than a whole head, will save you a few minutes prep in the kitchen.

# ROASTED BALSAMIC ASPARAGUS

Recipe by JOANNA SAYAGO GOLUB

**MAKES 4 SERVINGS**
**TOTAL TIME: 20 MINUTES**

- 1 bunch (1 pound) asparagus, trimmed
- 1 tablespoon extra-virgin olive oil
- ½ tablespoon balsamic vinegar
- ¼ teaspoon salt
- ¼ teaspoon ground black pepper

*Balsamic vinegar adds a touch of sweetness that's enhanced by roasting the asparagus.*

Preheat the oven to 425°F.

Spread the asparagus in a single layer on a baking sheet. Drizzle with the oil, vinegar, salt, and pepper. Toss well to coat and spread in a single layer again. Roast the asparagus for 15 to 18 minutes, until softened and slightly browned.

NUTRITION PER SERVING: 46 calories, 3 g carbs, 1 g fiber, 1 g protein, 4 g total fat, 0.5 g saturated fat, 147 mg sodium

# MASHED PROTEIN POTATOES

Recipe by LIZ APPLEGATE, PH.D.

**MAKES 6 SERVINGS**
**TOTAL TIME: 25 MINUTES**

- 3 pounds russet (baking) potatoes, unpeeled and cut into 1-inch cubes
- 1 cup 2% plain Greek yogurt
- 1 cup shredded Monterey jack cheese
- 2 tablespoons chopped fresh chives, flat-leaf parsley, or dill
- ¼ teaspoon salt
- ¼ teaspoon ground black pepper

*Using Greek yogurt instead of butter and cream not only saves you calories and fat, but also creates a creamier tasting dish with more protein than traditional mashed spuds. Leaving the skins on the potatoes makes for quicker prep—and adds fiber and rustic texture.*

In a medium pot, bring 1 inch of water to a boil over high heat. Add the potatoes and reduce the heat so that the water is at a moderate boil. Cover and cook, stirring once, for 15 to 20 minutes, until the potatoes are fork-tender. Drain the potatoes and return them to the pot. Add the yogurt, then roughly mash. Stir in the Monterey jack, chives, salt, and pepper.

NUTRITION PER SERVING: 275 calories, 43 g carbs, 3 g fiber, 13 g protein, 7 g total fat, 4 g saturated fat, 222 mg sodium

# SEAFOOD MAINS

## *Fish*

## *Shellfish*

# OVEN-FRIED FLOUNDER

**Recipe by THE RODALE TEST KITCHEN**

**MAKES 4 SERVINGS**
**TOTAL TIME: 20 MINUTES**

- 1 large egg
- 1 tablespoon water
- 1 cup whole wheat panko breadcrumbs
- 1 scallion, finely chopped
- 1 teaspoon dried tarragon or oregano
- ¼ teaspoon salt
- ¼ teaspoon ground black pepper
- 4 large flounder fillets (about 6 ounces each)
- 2 tablespoons extra-virgin olive oil
- 1 tablespoon butter, melted
- 4 lemon wedges

*A blast of high heat from the oven makes these fillets extra crispy—but without the need to use copious amounts of oil. For the most eco-friendly choice, look for wild-caught flounder from the U.S. Pacific coast. Serve with Broccoli with Lemon-Garlic Sauce (page 178).*

Position a rack in the top third of the oven and preheat to 500°F. Coat a baking dish (large enough to hold the fish in a single layer) with cooking spray.

In a shallow bowl, beat the egg with the water. In another shallow bowl, mix together the panko, scallion, tarragon, salt, and pepper.

Dip the fish in the egg and then coat with the crumb mixture, patting it on to adhere. Arrange the fish in the baking dish.

Drizzle the oil and butter over the fish. Bake for 5 to 8 minutes, until the fish just flakes when tested with a fork and the crust is golden brown. Serve with lemon wedges.

NUTRITION PER SERVING: 296 calories, 14 g carbs, 2 g fiber, 26 g protein, 15 g total fat, 4 g saturated fat, 715 mg sodium

# HALIBUT WITH LEMON-CAPER SAUCE

Recipe by THE RODALE TEST KITCHEN

**MAKES 6 SERVINGS**
**TOTAL TIME: 20 MINUTES**

- 1½ pounds halibut, cut into 6 portions
- ¼ teaspoon salt
- ⅛ teaspoon ground black pepper
- ½ cup all-purpose flour
- 4 tablespoons extra-virgin olive oil
- ¼ cup capers, drained
- 2 tablespoons chopped shallots
- 1 teaspoon grated lemon zest
- 3 tablespoons fresh lemon juice
- 4 tablespoons (½ stick) butter, cut into pieces
- 1 tablespoon chopped fresh flat-leaf parsley

*Halibut is a very firm, almost meaty fish with a mild flavor and creamy white color. It's a lean source of protein and provides omega-3 fatty acids. Wild Alaskan and Pacific halibut are both environmentally friendly choices. Serve with Mashed Protein Potatoes (page 179).*

Season the halibut on both sides with ⅛ teaspoon of the salt and the pepper. Place the flour in a shallow bowl or pie plate.

In a large skillet, heat 2 tablespoons of the oil over medium-high heat. Lightly coat half of the fish in the flour and place in the hot skillet. Cook, turning once, for 2 to 3 minutes, or until the fish just flakes when tested with a fork and the edges are golden brown. Transfer to a warm platter. Add another 1 tablespoon of oil to the skillet, if necessary, and repeat with the remaining fish. Transfer to the platter and cover to keep warm.

After the fish is cooked, add the remaining 1 tablespoon oil, the capers, and shallots to the skillet. Cook for 1 minute, or until the shallots are golden. Add the lemon zest and juice and bring to a simmer for about 30 seconds. Add the remaining ⅛ teaspoon salt and a pinch of pepper. Remove from the heat and add the butter and parsley, stirring until the butter melts.

Spoon the sauce over the fish and serve.

NUTRITION PER SERVING: 275 calories, 5 g carbs, 1 g fiber, 22 g protein, 18 g total fat, 6 g saturated fat, 335 mg sodium

**QUICK TIP** If you can't find fresh wild Alaskan or Pacific halibut, look for frozen fillets in the freezer aisle.

# THAI FISH CURRY

Recipe by THE RODALE TEST KITCHEN

**MAKES 4 SERVINGS**
**TOTAL TIME: 30 MINUTES**

- 2 tablespoons extra-virgin olive oil
- ½ yellow onion, sliced
- 2 teaspoons red curry paste
- 2 teaspoons turmeric
- 1 clove garlic, chopped
- ¼ teaspoon salt
- ¼ teaspoon ground black pepper
- 1 can (14.5 ounces) diced tomatoes
- 1 can (13.5 ounces) light coconut milk
- 1 cup frozen cut green beans
- 1½ pounds cod, cut into 1-inch chunks
- 1 lime, cut into wedges
- ¼ cup fresh cilantro, roughly chopped

*Firm, meaty cod is a good match for this fast, flavorful curry. Most Atlantic cod is imported from well-managed fisheries. Alaskan cod is also an eco-friendly choice. Red curry paste (made from a blend of chiles, herbs, and spices) is essential to any Thai curry. Look for it in the Asian aisle at most grocery stores. For a carb boost, serve over rice noodles or rice.*

In a large pot, heat the oil over medium-high heat. Add the onion and cook, stirring often, for 4 minutes, or until the onion is softened and golden.

Add the curry paste, turmeric, garlic, salt, and pepper. Stir for 1 minute, until well combined. Add the tomatoes (with their juices), coconut milk, and green beans. Bring to a simmer, then reduce the heat to medium-low and simmer for 4 minutes longer.

Add the cod and simmer for 5 minutes, or until the fish is opaque and just flakes when tested with a fork.

Divide the fish and broth among 4 bowls, squeeze a wedge of lime juice over, and top with chopped cilantro.

NUTRITION PER SERVING: 296 calories, 16 g carbs, 3 g fiber, 28 g protein, 13 g total fat, 5 g saturated fat, 1,019 mg sodium

**QUICK TIP** Stock your freezer with a range of unseasoned vegetables, like frozen cut green beans, so you can add them to quick dinners like this one.

# SMOKED SALMON PIZZA

Recipe by JENNIFER KUSHNIER

**MAKES 4 SERVINGS**
**TOTAL TIME: 15 MINUTES**

- 1 prebaked whole wheat pizza crust (10 ounces)
- 4 ounces cream cheese, at room temperature
- Juice of ½ lemon
- 2 tablespoons chopped fresh dill, plus more for garnish
- 2 tablespoons finely chopped red onion
- 1 tablespoon capers, drained
- 1½ teaspoons prepared horseradish
- ¼ teaspoon ground black pepper
- 4 ounces smoked salmon, roughly chopped

*Quick and convenient, smoked salmon shouldn't be limited to your break-fast menu. It requires no additional cooking and adds loads of flavor and protein to meals. The herbed cream cheese spread is the perfect balance to the salty, smoky fish. Serve with a green salad tossed with Fresh Herb Vinaigrette (page 101).*

Preheat the oven to 450°F.

Place the pizza crust on a baking sheet and bake for 5 minutes, or until the top is golden.

Meanwhile, in a bowl, with an electric mixer, beat together the cream cheese and lemon juice for 2 minutes, or until smooth and light. Stir in the dill, red onion, capers, horseradish, and pepper until well combined.

Remove the crust from the oven and spread the cream cheese mixture evenly across, leaving a ½- to 1-inch border. Scatter the salmon over the warm crust and garnish with extra dill.

NUTRITION PER SERVING: 380 calories, 35 g carbs, 6 g fiber, 27 g protein, 17 g total fat, 8 g saturated fat, 518 mg sodium

# HONEY-SOY GLAZED ARCTIC CHAR

**Recipe by THE RODALE TEST KITCHEN**

**MAKES 4 SERVINGS**
**TOTAL TIME: 20 MINUTES**

- 1½ pounds arctic char or salmon fillet, cut into 4 portions
- ¼ teaspoon ground black pepper
- 1 tablespoon soy sauce
- 1 tablespoon honey
- 1 tablespoon fresh lime juice, plus 1 teaspoon grated zest
- 2 scallions, chopped

*With its pink color, artic char resembles salmon but has a slightly milder flavor. Like salmon, it's a good source of omega-3 fatty acids, which help reduce inflammation. Most char available in the United States is farmed in an environmentally friendly way. Topping the fish with a honey-soy glaze brings out its natural sweetness. Serve with green beans and rice.*

Preheat the oven to 425°F. Coat a rimmed baking sheet with cooking spray.

Place the fish on the baking sheet and sprinkle with the pepper.

In a small bowl, stir together the soy sauce, honey, and lime juice. Drizzle half the glaze mixture over the fish fillets.

Roast the fish for 10 minutes, then drizzle with the remaining glaze. Roast for 5 to 8 minutes longer, until the fish just flakes when tested with a fork.

Serve the fish sprinkled with the scallions and lime zest.

NUTRITION PER SERVING: 372 calories, 4 g carbs, 1 g fiber, 36 g protein, 24 g fat, 1 g saturated fat, 395 sodium

# COCONUT MAHI-MAHI WITH PINEAPPLE SALSA

### Recipe by THE RODALE TEST KITCHEN

**MAKES 4 SERVINGS**
**TOTAL TIME: 25 MINUTES**

- 1 large egg
- 1 tablespoon water
- 1 cup unseasoned dried whole wheat breadcrumbs
- ⅓ cup unsweetened shredded coconut
- 1½ pounds mahi-mahi steaks, cut into 16 chunks
- ½ teaspoon salt
- ¼ teaspoon ground black pepper
- 3 tablespoons extra-virgin olive oil
- 1 can (15 ounces) juice-packed pineapple chunks, drained
- ¼ cup minced red bell pepper
- 2 scallions, thinly sliced
- 1 tablespoon honey
- 2 teaspoons fresh lime juice

*Rich, meaty mahi-mahi is a lean source of protein and energizing B vitamins. A 3-ounce serving provides 7 percent of your daily need for iron, which is key for maintaining endurance. For the most environmentally friendly choice, look for troll- or pole-caught wild mahi-mahi from the U.S. Atlantic. Serve with Basil-Mint Sugar Snaps (page 175).*

Preheat the oven to 375°F.

In a shallow bowl, beat the egg with the water. In another shallow bowl, combine the breadcrumbs and coconut.

Sprinkle the fish with the salt and pepper. Dip the fish in the egg mixture and then in the breadcrumb mixture until well coated. Pat to adhere.

Place the fish on a baking sheet and drizzle with the oil. Bake for 15 minutes, or until the crumbs are crisp and the fish chunks can be easily pierced with the tip of a knife.

Meanwhile, in a bowl, combine the pineapple, bell pepper, scallions, honey, and lime juice.

Serve the fish with the salsa on the side.

NUTRITION PER SERVING: 397 calories, 23 g carbs, 3 g fiber, 36 g protein, 18 g total fat, 6 g saturated fat, 519 mg sodium

**QUICK TIP** Feel free to substitute fresh pineapple for canned. Many grocery stores sell already cleaned and cut fresh pineapple chunks in the produce section, saving you the time and hassle of prepping a whole fruit yourself.

# BROILED TILAPIA WITH MANGO CHUTNEY

**Recipe by THE RODALE TEST KITCHEN**

**MAKES 4 SERVINGS**
**TOTAL TIME: 15 MINUTES**

- 2½ teaspoons paprika
- 2 teaspoons ground coriander
- ¾ teaspoon salt
- 4 tilapia fillets (about 6 ounces each)
- 1 teaspoon curry powder
- 1 large mango, cut into ½-inch chunks (about 1½ cups)
- 1 avocado, cut into ½-inch chunks
- ⅓ cup chopped fresh cilantro
- 2 tablespoons fresh lime juice
- 2 teaspoons extra-virgin olive oil
- 6 cups baby arugula (about 5 ounces)

*Mild-tasting, quick-cooking tilapia is the perfect base for a full-flavored, fresh Indian chutney. Tank-farmed tilapia from the United States or Canada and pond-raised fish from Ecuador are the most environmentally friendly choices. When paired with 10-minute brown rice, this dish can work for a prerun or recovery meal.*

Position an oven rack 6 inches from the heat and preheat the broiler to high. Coat a broilerproof pan with cooking spray.

In a large bowl, stir together the paprika, coriander, and salt. Place the fillets on the pan and sprinkle with 2 teaspoons of the spice mixture, rubbing it into the fish. Broil the tilapia, without turning, for 5 minutes, or until the fish just flakes when tested with a fork.

Meanwhile, to the spice mixture remaining in the bowl, add the curry powder, mango, avocado, cilantro, lime juice, and oil. Toss to combine.

Divide the arugula among 4 plates. Top it with the tilapia and chutney.

NUTRITION PER SERVING: 281 calories, 18 g carbs, 5 g fiber, 34 g protein, 10 g total fat, 2 g saturated fat, 509 mg sodium

# LETTUCE-WRAPPED ASIAN SALMON BURGERS

Recipe by MATTHEW KADEY, M.S., R.D.

**MAKES 4 SERVINGS**
**TOTAL TIME: 30 MINUTES**

- 1 pound skinless salmon fillet
- 2 tablespoons soy sauce
- 1 tablespoon Sriracha or other chili-garlic sauce
- 2 cloves garlic, chopped
- 2 teaspoons finely chopped fresh ginger
- ¼ teaspoon ground black pepper
- ¼ cup toasted wheat germ
- 3 scallions, chopped
- ⅓ cup chopped fresh cilantro
- 1 tablespoon canola oil
- 4 fresh or canned pineapple rings
- 4 large lettuce leaves, such as Bibb, Boston, or other butter lettuce
- 2 tablespoons hoisin sauce

*The surprise ingredient in these sweet and savory burgers is wheat germ. It serves as a binder, taking the place of less-nutritious breadcrumbs, and provides fiber, B vitamins, and zinc—needed for immune function. Grilled pineapple makes for a juicy topping that's abundant in vitamin C and manganese. You can wrap the burgers in any soft, pliable lettuce leaves.*

Preheat a grill or grill pan to medium heat.

In a food processor, combine ½ pound of the salmon, the soy sauce, Sriracha, garlic, ginger, and pepper. Process until pureed and pasty.

Finely chop the remaining ½ pound of salmon by hand. Pulse it into the pureed mixture, along with the wheat germ, scallions, and cilantro. Shape into 4 patties.

Brush the grill grates or grill pan with ½ tablespoon of the oil. Transfer the patties to the grill and cook for 3 to 4 minutes per side, or until they reach an internal temperature of 140°F.

Brush the pineapple rings with the remaining ½ tablespoon oil. Grill for 2 minutes per side, or until they have grill marks.

Place each burger on a lettuce leaf and top with hoisin sauce and a pineapple ring. Wrap the lettuce around the burger and serve.

NUTRITION PER SERVING: 412 calories, 31 g carbs, 2 g fiber, 29 g protein, 20 g total fat, 4 g saturated fat, 737 mg sodium

# SALMON CUPS WITH AVOCADO SAUCE

Recipe by MATTHEW KADEY, M.S., R.D.

**MAKES 5 SERVINGS**
**TOTAL TIME: 30 MINUTES**

## Salmon Cups

- 2 cans (6 ounces each) wild salmon, drained
- 2 large eggs
- ½ cup whole wheat breadcrumbs
- ⅓ cup 2% milk
- 1 large zucchini (10 ounces), shredded
- 1 teaspoon curry powder
- ¼ teaspoon salt
- ¼ teaspoon ground black pepper

## Sauce

- ½ avocado
- ¼ cup plain low-fat yogurt
- Juice of ½ lime
- ½ teaspoon wasabi paste or powder (optional)
- ⅛ teaspoon salt

*Canned salmon is one of the richest sources of the omega-3 fats EPA and DHA. These fats decrease heart-disease risk and improve bone strength, which may help runners avoid stress fractures. They're also an excellent source of protein and vitamin D. Some canned salmon comes with the bones, which are edible—but boneless varieties are also available. Serve with a mixed greens salad.*

Preheat the oven to 350°F. Lightly coat 10 cups of a muffin tin with cooking spray.

For the salmon cups: In a large bowl, combine the salmon, eggs, breadcrumbs, milk, zucchini, curry powder, salt, and pepper. Mix until well combined.

Use a ⅓-cup measuring cup to scoop the mixture and fill the 10 muffin cups. Bake for 20 minutes, or until puffed and set. Let sit in the muffin tin for 1 minute before removing.

Meanwhile, make the sauce: In a food processor, combine the avocado, yogurt, lime juice, wasabi (if using), and salt. Process until smooth.

Serve the salmon cups with the avocado sauce.

NUTRITION PER SERVING: 253 calories, 14 g carbs, 3 g fiber, 26 g protein, 11 g total fat, 2.5 g saturated fat, 713 mg sodium

# BAKED MACKEREL IN SPICY TOMATO-CHICKPEA SAUCE

Recipe by THE RODALE TEST KITCHEN

**MAKES 4 SERVINGS**
**TOTAL TIME: 30 MINUTES**

- 4 skin-on Spanish mackerel fillets (5 ounces each, from two 1-pound fish)
- 1 tablespoons extra-virgin olive oil
- 2 cloves garlic, thinly sliced
- ½ teaspoon red pepper flakes
- 1 can (14.5 ounces) crushed tomatoes
- ¾ teaspoon ground cumin
- ¾ teaspoon chili powder
- ½ teaspoon dried oregano
- ½ teaspoon salt
- 1 can (15 ounces) chickpeas, drained and rinsed

*Spanish mackerel is a sustainable and inexpensive fish that is extremely rich in inflammation-reducing omega-3 fatty acids, making it an ideal choice for runners. While the Spanish variety has a milder flavor than others, it's a bold fish and needs an equally robust sauce to go with it. This spicy tomato number does the job perfectly.*

Preheat the oven to 425°F. Coat a shallow baking pan with cooking spray.

Place the fish in the baking pan.

In a large skillet, heat the oil over medium heat. Add the garlic and pepper flakes and cook for 1 minute, or until the garlic starts to turn golden.

Add the tomatoes, cumin, chili powder, oregano, and salt and simmer for 1 minute. Stir in the chickpeas and cook for 1 minute to heat through.

Pour the sauce over and around the fish. Bake for 13 to 15 minutes, until the fish just flakes when tested with a fork.

NUTRITION PER SERVING: 422 calories, 28 g carbs, 7 g fiber, 41 g protein, 16 g total fat, 4 g saturated fat, 532 mg sodium

**QUICK TIP** Spanish mackerel are typically only available whole, so ask at the fish counter to have them filleted for you. Don't substitute king mackerel, which can contain high levels of mercury.

# BROILED GARLICKY SHRIMP

Recipe by THE RODALE TEST KITCHEN

**MAKES 6 SERVINGS**
**TOTAL TIME: 15 MINUTES**

- 3 tablespoons butter, melted
- 2 tablespoons extra-virgin olive oil
- 2 tablespoons fresh lemon juice
- 2 large cloves garlic, minced
- ½ teaspoon salt
- ¼ teaspoon ground black pepper
- 2 pounds (26 to 30 count) large shrimp, peeled and deveined
- 2 tablespoons chopped fresh flat-leaf parsley, for serving

*Leave the tails on the shrimp. It cuts down on prep work and makes for a nice presentation. Serve with Broccoli with Lemon-Garlic Sauce (page 178) and whole wheat orzo on the side.*

Position an oven rack in the highest position and preheat the broiler to high. Line a broiler pan with foil.

In a large bowl, combine the melted butter, oil, lemon juice, garlic, salt, and pepper. Add the shrimp and stir until well coated.

Remove the shrimp from the butter mixture and arrange in a single layer on the broiler pan. Pour the butter mixture remaining in the bowl over all the shrimp. Broil for 2 minutes. Turn with tongs and broil for 2 to 3 minutes longer, or until the shrimp are opaque throughout.

Transfer, with the cooking juices, to a serving platter and sprinkle with the parsley.

NUTRITION PER SERVING: 189 calories, 2 g carbs, 0 g fiber, 18 g protein, 12 g total fat, 4.5 g saturated fat, 994 mg sodium

# STIR-FRIED TOFU AND SHRIMP

Recipe by MARK BITTMAN

**MAKES 4 SERVINGS**
**TOTAL TIME: 15 MINUTES**

- 2 tablespoons peanut oil or canola oil
- 3 ounces presliced shiitake mushrooms (about 1 cup)
- 1 tablespoon chopped garlic
- 1 tablespoon chopped fresh ginger
- 6 ounces snow peas (about 2 cups)
- 1 package (16 ounces) extra-firm tofu, drained and cut into 1-inch cubes
- ½ pound peeled and deveined medium shrimp
- ¼ cup white wine or sherry
- ⅓ cup low-sodium vegetable broth or water
- 2 tablespoons soy sauce
- ½ cup chopped scallions, white parts only

*This high-protein dish created by* Runner's World *contributing food writer Mark Bittman contains a healthy dose of vegetables. Like most stir-fries, it's really fast to make, so have all your ingredients prepped before you start cooking. Add a bowl of rice to make it ideal for a prerun meal.*

In a large skillet or wok, heat 1 tablespoon of the oil over high heat. When hot, add the mushrooms and cook for 5 minutes, stirring occasionally, until browned and almost crisp. Remove with a slotted spoon and set aside.

Add the remaining 1 tablespoon oil to the pan, followed by the garlic and ginger. Cook, stirring constantly, for 10 seconds. Add the snow peas and continue to cook, stirring occasionally, for 3 minutes, or until they turn bright green and soften slightly.

Add the tofu and shrimp and cook, stirring occasionally, for 2 to 3 minutes, or until the shrimp turns pink. Add the wine and broth. Cook, stirring occasionally, until about half of the liquid evaporates.

Return the mushrooms to the skillet and cook, stirring often, for 1 minute, or until reheated. Add the soy sauce and scallions. Cook, stirring often, for 30 seconds, or until the scallions become glossy.

NUTRITION PER SERVING: 277 calories, 13 g carbs, 5 g fiber, 25 g protein, 14 g total fat, 3 g saturated fat, 920 mg sodium

# CURRY CRAB BURGERS

Recipe by MATTHEW KADEY, M.S., R.D.

**MAKES 4 SERVINGS**
**TOTAL TIME: 20 MINUTES**

- 1 pound pasteurized lump crabmeat
- ¾ cup fresh or thawed frozen corn kernels
- ½ cup whole wheat panko breadcrumbs
- 1 large egg
- 3 tablespoons mayonnaise
- 2 tablespoons chopped fresh chives
- 2 teaspoons Dijon mustard
- 1½ teaspoons curry powder
- ¼ teaspoon ground black pepper
- 1 teaspoon extra-virgin olive oil
- 4 ciabatta rolls
- 4 tablespoons guacamole, such as Liz's Famous Guacamole (page 57)

*Just 3 ounces of crab provides more than 100 percent of your daily need for vitamin B$_{12}$. This nutrient plays a role in producing red blood cells, which help carry oxygen to muscles. Runners who don't get enough vitamin B$_{12}$ may fatigue more easily. Crab is also rich in selenium, an antioxidant that may reduce levels of oxidative stress following exercise, which could help speed recovery. In addition to the guacamole, top the burgers with lettuce and tomato, if desired.*

Preheat a grill pan over medium-high heat.

In a large bowl, combine the crabmeat, corn, breadcrumbs, egg, mayonnaise, chives, mustard, curry powder, and pepper. Mix well. Shape the mixture into 4 patties.

Brush the oil on the grill pan. Carefully place the burgers on the pan and cook for 5 minutes per side.

Place the burgers on the rolls and top each with 1 tablespoon guacamole.

NUTRITION PER SERVING: 475 calories, 45 g carbs, 3 g fiber, 35 g protein, 15 g total fat, 2 g saturated fat, 922 mg sodium

**QUICK TIP** These burgers are also delicious as sliders—just form the mixture into about 15 patties instead of 4.

# MUSSELS WITH WHITE WINE AND SHALLOTS

Recipe by THE RODALE TEST KITCHEN

**MAKES 4 SERVINGS**
**TOTAL TIME: 15 MINUTES**

- 4 pounds mussels
- 2 tablespoons extra-virgin olive oil
- 4 shallots, minced (about 1 cup)
- 3 cloves garlic, minced
- 1 cup dry white wine
- ¼ cup chopped fresh flat-leaf parsley

*Inexpensive, tasty, and easy to prepare, mussels are a good source of protein and iron, providing 32 percent of your daily need in 3 ounces. They're also a good source of zinc, which plays a role in maintaining a healthy immune system. Serve with salad greens and fresh, crusty bread to dip in the flavorful broth.*

Put the mussels in a large colander set in the sink. Rinse with cool water. Sort through them and discard any that have cracked shells. Pull off any stringy growth—this is the mussel's "beard"—protruding from between the shells near the hinge. (Most farmed mussels are debearded before being sold, so you may be able to skip this step.)

In a 6-quart pot, heat the oil over low heat. Add the shallots and garlic, and cook, stirring occasionally, for 5 minutes, or until the shallots are tender. Add the wine, increase the heat to high, and bring to a boil. Add the mussels, cover the pan, and cook for 5 to 7 minutes, or until the mussels have opened. Discard any that do not open.

Spoon the mussels into 4 serving bowls. Stir the parsley into the broth in the pot and spoon over the mussels.

NUTRITION PER SERVING: 439 calories, 28 g carbs, 0 g fiber, 41 g protein, 14 g total fat, 2 g saturated fat, 914 mg sodium

QUICK TIP This recipe works equally well with littleneck clams: Use 3 to 4 dozen clams in place of the mussels.

# SEARED SCALLOPS WITH BABY SPINACH

### Recipe by THE RODALE TEST KITCHEN

**MAKES 4 SERVINGS**
**TOTAL TIME: 15 MINUTES**

- 1 pound sea scallops, side tendon removed
- ¼ cup all-purpose flour
- ½ teaspoon salt
- ½ teaspoon ground black pepper
- 1 tablespoon canola oil
- 1 tablespoon butter
- 1 lemon, halved
- 10 ounces baby spinach
- 2 tablespoons chopped fresh flat-leaf parsley

*Sweet, tender, and quick cooking, scallops look impressive but couldn't be simpler to serve on a busy weeknight. There are two basic types—sea scallops (used here), which are quite large, and bay scallops, which are much smaller and too delicate to sear. When shopping, look for farmed scallops, which are easy to find and are an eco-friendly choice, thanks to sustainable farming practices worldwide. Serve with Sweet Potato Pumpkin Seed Salad (page 85). Or pair with rice for a prerun meal.*

Dry the scallops well with paper towels. In a medium bowl, mix together the flour, salt, and pepper. Add the scallops and toss to lightly coat.

In a large skillet, heat the oil and butter over medium heat until the butter has melted. Add the scallops and cook, without turning, for 2 to 3 minutes, or until the scallops have formed a deep golden crust. Flip the scallops and squeeze the juice from a lemon half over them. Cook for 2 minutes on the second side, until the scallops are golden, just opaque, and slightly firm when pressed. Transfer to a plate and cover to keep warm.

Return the skillet to medium heat and add the spinach and juice from the remaining lemon half. Cook, stirring often with tongs, for 1 to 2 minutes, or until the spinach is lightly cooked and wilted. Add a splash of water, if needed to prevent the skillet from drying.

Divide the spinach among 4 plates, top with the scallops, then sprinkle with the parsley.

NUTRITION PER SERVING: 174 calories, 14 g carbs, 4 g fiber, 16 g protein, 7 g total fat, 2 g saturated fat, 874 mg sodium

QUICK TIP Sea scallops are typically sold with their side tendon still attached. Simply peel it off with your fingers before cooking.

# MEAT and POULTRY MAINS

### *Meat*

### *Poultry*

# SPICE-RUBBED FLANK STEAK WITH CHILE-TOMATO SALSA

Recipe by THE RODALE TEST KITCHEN

**MAKES 4 SERVINGS**
**TOTAL TIME: 30 MINUTES**

- 1 tablespoon plus 1 teaspoon ground cumin
- 3 cloves garlic, minced
- 3 tablespoons fresh lime juice
- 1 teaspoon ground black pepper
- ¾ teaspoon salt
- 1¼ pounds flank steak or top round steak, trimmed of all visible fat
- 1 large tomato, finely chopped
- 1 can (4.5 ounces) chopped mild green chilies, drained
- ¼ red onion, diced

*A lean and quick-cooking cut of beef, flank steak is a protein- and iron-rich choice for runners. Because it's so lean, it's best served medium-rare so that it retains its flavorful juices. Pair it with Summer Corn Salad (page 76).*

Lightly oil a grill rack or broiler-pan rack. Preheat the grill or broiler.

In a small skillet, stir the cumin over medium heat for 3 minutes, or until fragrant and darker in color. Transfer to a small bowl to cool. Measure out 1 teaspoon of the toasted cumin and place in a medium bowl.

To the small bowl, add the garlic, 2 tablespoons of the lime juice, the black pepper, and ½ teaspoon of the salt and mix well. Place the steak on the prepared rack and rub the cumin-garlic mixture over both sides of the steak. Let stand at room temperature while you make the salsa.

In the medium bowl with the reserved cumin, combine the tomato, chilies, onion, and the remaining 1 tablespoon lime juice and ¼ teaspoon salt. Let the salsa stand at room temperature until serving.

Grill or broil the steak for 4 minutes per side, or until the center of the steak reaches an internal temperature of 145°F for medium-rare.

Let the steak rest on a cutting board for 5 minutes before thinly slicing against the grain.

Serve the steak topped with the salsa.

NUTRITION PER SERVING: 266 calories, 6 g carbs, 2 g fiber, 31 g protein, 12 g total fat, 5 g saturated fat, 632 mg sodium

# GINGERED BEEF WITH BROCCOLINI AND CASHEWS

Recipe by THE RODALE TEST KITCHEN

**MAKES 4 SERVINGS**
**TOTAL TIME: 20 MINUTES**

- 2 tablespoons oyster sauce
- 2 tablespoons finely chopped fresh ginger
- 1 tablespoon reduced-sodium soy sauce
- 1 teaspoon chili-garlic sauce or Sriracha
- 2 tablespoons plus ¼ cup water
- 1 tablespoon toasted sesame oil
- 1½ pounds broccolini, trimmed and cut into bite-size pieces
- ¾ pound flank steak, cut into thin strips against the grain
- 1 bunch scallions, cut into 1-inch pieces
- ¼ cup unsalted roasted cashew pieces, roughly chopped

*Look for oyster sauce and chili-garlic sauce in the Asian aisle of most supermarkets. Both ingredients punch up the flavor in this simple stir-fry. Serve the dish with 10-minute brown rice.*

In a small bowl, whisk together the oyster sauce, ginger, soy sauce, chili-garlic sauce, and 2 tablespoons of the water. Set aside.

In a wok or large skillet, heat the sesame oil over medium-high heat. Add the broccolini and cook for 3 minutes. Add the remaining ¼ cup water and cook for 2 minutes longer. Add the steak, scallions, and oyster sauce mixture. Cook for 2 to 3 minutes, or until the beef is just cooked through. Stir in the cashews and serve immediately.

NUTRITION PER SERVING: 292 calories, 19 g carbs, 3 g fiber, 27 g protein, 12 g total fat, 3 g saturated fat, 548 mg sodium

**QUICK TIP** You can substitute 2 additional tablespoons of soy sauce plus 1 teaspoon sugar for the oyster sauce.

# SOFT BEEF TACOS

Recipe by THE RODALE TEST KITCHEN

**MAKES 4 SERVINGS**
**TOTAL TIME: 25 MINUTES**

- 1 teaspoon paprika
- ½ teaspoon chili powder
- ½ teaspoon onion powder
- ¼ teaspoon salt
- ¼ teaspoon ground black pepper
- ¾ pound top sirloin, cut into thin strips
- Juice of 1 lime
- ½ tablespoon canola oil
- 1 cup chopped red bell pepper
- 3 cloves garlic, minced
- 2 chipotle peppers in adobo sauce, minced
- ½ cup salsa
- 8 soft flour tortillas (6 to 8 inches)
- 1 cup shredded Monterey jack cheese (4 ounces)
- ¼ cup sour cream
- ¼ cup chopped fresh cilantro

*Rich in carbs and protein, these tacos provide everything you need to recover from a tough run. Chipotle peppers pack a spicy punch, so use mild salsa if you don't want to increase the heat further.*

In a small bowl, combine the paprika, chili powder, onion powder, salt, and black pepper. Place the beef in a plastic zip-top bag and add the spice mixture. Shake well to coat the beef. Add the lime juice and shake again. Refrigerate the meat until ready to cook.

In a large skillet, heat the oil over medium heat. Add the bell pepper and garlic and cook, stirring often, for 3 minutes, or until the bell pepper is softened. Transfer to a plate and set aside.

Add the beef and cook, stirring often, for 5 minutes, or until cooked through. Return the bell pepper mixture to the pan along with the chipotles and salsa. Cook, stirring often, for 2 minutes to heat through and thoroughly combine.

Wrap the tortillas in a damp paper towel and microwave on high for 1 minute.

Place a portion of the beef mixture down the center of each tortilla. Top with the cheese, sour cream, and cilantro.

NUTRITION PER SERVING: 407 calories, 31 g carbs, 3 g fiber, 29 g protein, 19 g total fat, 8.5 g saturated fat, 529 mg sodium

# STEAK AND PEPPER RICE BOWL

Recipe by MATTHEW KADEY, M.S., R.D.

**MAKES 4 SERVINGS**
**TOTAL TIME: 30 MINUTES**

## Rice Bowl

- 2 cups 10-minute brown rice
- 1 pound top sirloin steak, ¾ inch thick, trimmed of visible fat
- ¼ teaspoon salt
- ¼ teaspoon ground black pepper
- 3 teaspoons canola oil
- 2 red bell peppers, sliced
- 2 cups frozen corn kernels, thawed
- 2 tablespoons chopped fresh cilantro

## Sauce

- ½ cup reduced-fat sour cream
- Juice of ½ lime
- ½ avocado
- 1 clove garlic, roughly chopped
- ½ teaspoon ground cumin
- ¼ teaspoon chili powder
- ¼ teaspoon salt
- ¼ teaspoon ground black pepper

*Top sirloin steak is a lean cut of beef that provides easily absorbed, energy-boosting iron. Serving it over brown rice (along with a charred pepper-and-corn combo) provides additional carbs and antioxidants.*

Position an oven rack 4 inches from the heat and preheat the broiler to high.

For the rice bowl: Cook the brown rice according to the package directions.

Meanwhile, season the steak on both sides with the salt and pepper, then rub with 1 teaspoon of the oil. Place the steak on a broilerproof pan and cook about 10 minutes, flipping halfway through with tongs, or until it reaches an internal temperature of 125°F for medium-rare.

Meanwhile, make the sauce: In a blender, combine the sour cream, lime juice, avocado, garlic, cumin, chili powder, salt, and pepper. Blend until smooth.

When the steak is done, let it rest for 5 minutes (it will finish cooking while it rests), then thinly slice.

While the steak rests, in a large skillet, heat the remaining 2 teaspoons oil over medium-high heat. Add the bell peppers and cook 2 minutes, stirring occasionally, until softened and beginning to brown. Add the corn and cook until slightly charred and heated through, about 1 minute longer.

Divide the cooked rice among 4 bowls. Top each with an even portion of steak and the bell pepper mixture. Drizzle with the sauce and top with the cilantro.

NUTRITION PER SERVING: 487 calories, 55 g carbs, 6 g fiber, 33 g protein, 17 g total fat, 5 g saturated fat, 394 mg sodium

**QUICK TIP** To ensure that the steak cooks quickly, take it out of the refrigerator as soon as you start prepping ingredients so that it has a chance to come to room temperature before going under the broiler.

# CHIPOTLE-COCOA BISON BURGERS

Recipe by MATTHEW KADEY, M.S., R.D.

**MAKES 4 SERVINGS**
**TOTAL TIME: 20 MINUTES**

- 1 pound ground bison or extra-lean (95%) ground beef
- 3 tablespoons barbecue sauce (plus more for serving, optional)
- 2 tablespoons unsweetened cocoa powder
- 2 chipotle peppers in adobo sauce, chopped
- 2 cloves garlic, minced
- 1 shallot, chopped
- 1 teaspoon ground cumin
- ¼ teaspoon salt
- ¼ teaspoon ground black pepper
- 4 slices provolone cheese
- 4 whole wheat hamburger rolls

*Bison tastes similar to beef but has a leaner fat profile and a slightly sweeter taste. Cocoa powder adds both flavor and a shot of antioxidants that help fend off cell-damaging free radicals. Top with any of your favorite hamburger fixings, including lettuce, tomato, red onion, and (for additional spice) sliced jalapeños.*

Brush a grill rack or grill pan with oil. Preheat the grill to medium-high heat or the grill pan over medium heat.

In a large bowl, add the bison, barbecue sauce, cocoa powder, chipotles, garlic, shallot, cumin, salt, and black pepper. Mix until thoroughly combined. Shape into 4 patties ½ inch thick.

Grill the burgers for about 4 minutes per side, or until the center reaches an internal temperature of 140°F. Top each burger with a slice of cheese and cook for 30 seconds, or until the cheese melts.

Remove the burgers from the grill and place each on a roll. If desired, top with additional barbecue sauce.

NUTRITION PER SERVING: 435 calories, 34 g carbs, 5 g fiber, 31 g protein, 20 g total fat, 8 g saturated fat, 813 mg sodium

# INDIAN-SPICED BONELESS PORK CHOPS

**Recipe by THE RODALE TEST KITCHEN**

**MAKES 4 SERVINGS**
**TOTAL TIME: 15 MINUTES**

2 teaspoons garam masala

1 teaspoon sugar

½ teaspoon salt

½ teaspoon ground cinnamon

4 boneless pork loin chops, ¾ inch thick (5 ounces each)

4 teaspoons canola oil

*If you're stuck in a chicken breast rut, try boneless pork loin chops for a change. They're lean and mild tasting, so they easily meld with sweet or savory flavors—both of which are in the garam masala spice rub used here. Serve with Spiced Chickpeas with Spinach (page 166) for a side.*

Position an oven rack 4 inches from the heat and preheat the broiler to high.

In a small bowl, combine the garam masala, sugar, salt, and cinnamon. Rub the mixture all over the chops, then rub with the oil.

Place the chops on a broilerproof baking sheet and cook for 3 minutes per side, or until the pork reaches an internal temperature of 145°F. Allow the chops to rest for 3 minutes before serving.

NUTRITION PER SERVING: 256 calories, 0 g carbs, 0 g fiber, 31 g protein, 14 g total fat, 4 g saturated fat, 354 mg sodium

# MEDITERRANEAN PORK FLATBREADS

Recipe by THE RODALE TEST KITCHEN

**MAKES 4 SERVINGS**
**TOTAL TIME: 25 MINUTES**

- 1 tablespoon plus 2 teaspoons extra-virgin olive oil
- ½ pound pork tenderloin, thinly sliced crosswise
- 4 whole wheat naan flatbreads
- ½ cup store-bought olive tapenade
- ½ cup crumbled blue cheese (2 ounces)
- 1 cup thinly sliced fennel
- 2 tablespoons chopped walnuts
- 1 cup baby arugula

*Pork tenderloin is an exceptionally lean cut of meat. It has a 6:1 ratio of protein to fat calories, along with a high amount of selenium, an antioxidant that may ease exercise-induced oxidative stress in the body.*

Preheat the oven to 400°F. Line 2 baking sheets with parchment paper or foil.

In a large skillet, heat 1 tablespoon of the oil over medium heat. Add the pork and cook for 3 minutes, or until just cooked through and barely pink. Set aside.

Set the flatbreads on the baking sheets. Brush a ½-inch border all around the flatbreads with the remaining 2 teaspoons oil.

Spread the tapenade over the flatbreads, leaving the ½-inch border uncovered. Top with the pork, blue cheese, fennel, and walnuts. Bake for 9 to 10 minutes, until the crust is golden and crisp. Top the cooked flatbreads with the arugula and return to the oven for 1 minute longer.

NUTRITION PER SERVING: 369 calories, 32 g carbs, 6 g fiber, 16 g protein, 19 g total fat, 4.5 g saturated fat, 632 mg sodium

QUICK TIP Look for premade tapenade in the deli section or condiments aisle at the grocery store.

# BROILED LAMB CHOPS WITH SPINACH AND WHITE BEAN SAUTÉ

Recipe by THE RODALE TEST KITCHEN

**MAKES 4 SERVINGS**
**TOTAL TIME: 30 MINUTES**

1 tablespoon extra-virgin olive oil

1 large onion, thinly sliced

2 teaspoons sugar

1 teaspoon chopped fresh rosemary or ½ teaspoon dried

3 cloves garlic, sliced

¾ cup low-sodium beef broth

1 can (15 ounces) cannellini beans, drained and rinsed

6 cups baby spinach (about 5 ounces)

¼ teaspoon plus ⅛ teaspoon salt

¼ teaspoon ground black pepper

4 loin lamb chops (3 to 4 ounces each), trimmed of all visible fat

½ teaspoon fennel seeds, crushed

*Most of the fat in lamb is easily trimmed off before cooking, making it a lean, flavorful protein choice that's also a good source of vitamin B$_{12}$ and niacin. Pairing the meat with a quick bean sauté makes for a complete meal.*

Position an oven rack 4 inches from the heat and preheat the broiler to high. Coat a broiler pan with cooking spray.

In a large skillet, heat the oil over medium-high heat. Add the onion, sugar, and rosemary and cook for 7 minutes, stirring occasionally, or until starting to brown. Add the garlic and cook for 2 minutes.

Stir in the broth, bring to a boil, and cook for 1 minute. Stir in the beans and cook for 2 minutes. Add the spinach and cook for 1 minute, stirring, or until wilted. Remove from the heat and stir in ¼ teaspoon of the salt and ⅛ teaspoon of the pepper. Keep warm.

Sprinkle the lamb chops with the fennel seeds and remaining ⅛ teaspoon salt and ⅛ teaspoon pepper. Place on the broiler pan and broil for 6 minutes, turning once, or until browned and the center reaches an internal temperature of 145°F for medium-rare.

Serve with the bean mixture.

NUTRITION PER SERVING: 262 calories, 21 g carbs, 6 g fiber, 24 g protein, 9 g total fat, 2.5 g saturated fat, 530 mg sodium

**QUICK TIP** You don't need a spice grinder to crush fennel seeds. Simply press the bottom edge of a small, heavy pot into the seeds and slowly move the pot back and forth over the seeds to crush them. Or use the flat side of a chef's knife and press down on the blade to crush the seeds.

# SUNNY SIDE UP PIZZA

### Recipe by MATTHEW KADEY, M.S., R.D.

**MAKES 4 SERVINGS**
**TOTAL TIME: 25 MINUTES**

- 1 prebaked whole wheat pizza crust (10 ounces)
- 1 teaspoon extra-virgin olive oil
- ½ cup tomato sauce, such as Make-Ahead Tomato Sauce (page 156), or any jarred tomato sauce, warmed
- 1 cup baby spinach or chopped kale
- 1 cup shredded Havarti or part-skim mozzarella cheese (4 ounces)
- 2 slices Canadian bacon, diced
- 4 large eggs
- 1 tablespoon chopped fresh chives

*Ham and eggs may be traditional breakfast partners, but they taste even better tossed on this easy pizza and eaten any time of day. Both ingredients provide a good dose of protein, making this a recovery-friendly pie, too.*

Preheat the oven to 450°F.

Set the crust on a baking sheet and brush a 1-inch border of oil around the edges.

Spread the tomato sauce over the dough, leaving the 1-inch border uncovered. Top with the spinach, Havarti or mozzarella, and Canadian bacon.

Make 4 nests in the toppings and carefully crack 1 egg into each nest. Bake for 12 to 15 minutes, or until the egg whites are set but the yolks are still runny.

Serve garnished with the chives.

NUTRITION PER SERVING: 438 calories, 35 g carbs, 6 g fiber, 24 g protein, 23 g total fat, 11 g saturated fat, 824 mg sodium

# SKILLET HOPPIN' JOHN

Recipe by MARK BITTMAN

**MAKES 4 SERVINGS**
**TOTAL TIME: 30 MINUTES**

- 2 tablespoons extra-virgin olive oil
- 4 ounces slab bacon or smoked ham, cubed
- 2 onions, chopped
- 2 red bell peppers, chopped
- 2 cloves garlic, minced
- 1 tablespoon chopped fresh rosemary or thyme, or 1 teaspoon dried
- ⅛ teaspoon salt
- ⅛ teaspoon ground black pepper
- 2 cups cooked and chilled brown rice
- 2 cups cooked or canned black-eyed peas, drained, liquid reserved
- 2 teaspoons chopped fresh flat-leaf parsley

*This stir-fried version of the classic Southern dish "gets a ton of flavor from bits of bacon or ham, instead of a one-pound ham hock," says* Runner's World *contributing food writer Mark Bittman. It's a great way to use up leftovers. Add whatever vegetables and grains you have on hand.*

In a large skillet, heat the oil over medium-high heat. Add the bacon or ham and cook, stirring occasionally, for 5 to 10 minutes, or until the pieces are crisp and browned. Pour off all but 2 tablespoons of the fat and reduce the heat to medium. (If you're using smoked ham, which is very lean, you won't need to pour off any fat.)

Add the onions, bell peppers, and garlic to the skillet and cook, stirring occasionally, for 5 to 10 minutes, until soft and browned. Stir in the rosemary or thyme, salt, and black pepper.

Begin to add the rice, a bit at a time, breaking up any clumps and stirring it into the oil. When all the rice has been added and is glossy, add the black-eyed peas with ½ cup of their liquid. Cook, stirring often, for 1 to 2 minutes, until heated through.

Serve sprinkled with the parsley.

NUTRITION PER SERVING: 407 calories, 45 g carbs, 7 g fiber, 13 g protein, 20 g total fat, 5 g saturated fat, 308 mg sodium

# SWEET AND SPICY CHICKEN STIR-FRY

Recipe by MATTHEW KADEY, M.S., R.D.

**MAKES 4 SERVINGS**
**TOTAL TIME: 25 MINUTES**

- 2 cups 10-minute brown rice
- 1 tablespoon plus 1 teaspoon canola oil
- 1½ pounds boneless, skinless chicken breast, cut into ¾-inch cubes
- ¼ teaspoon salt
- ¼ teaspoon ground black pepper
- 1 red bell pepper, cut into ¼-inch-wide strips
- 1½ cups frozen mango slices or chunks, thawed
- 2 tablespoons soy sauce
- 1 tablespoon finely chopped fresh ginger
- ½ teaspoon red pepper flakes
- Juice of 1 lime
- 3 scallions, sliced

*Frozen mango slices add tropical flare to your diet, minus the hassle of peeling and slicing the fresh fruit. Research shows that antioxidants in mango may have anticancer properties that inhibit tumor cell growth. For less spice, start with ¼ teaspoon red pepper flakes and taste before adding more.*

Prepare the brown rice according to the package directions.

Meanwhile, in a large skillet, heat the oil over medium-high heat. Season the chicken with the salt and pepper, then add to the skillet. Cook, stirring occasionally, for 4 to 5 minutes, until the chicken is no longer pink. Add the bell pepper and cook, stirring occasionally, for 2 minutes, or until the pepper starts to soften.

Reduce the heat to medium. Add the mango, soy sauce, ginger, pepper flakes, and lime juice. Cook for 3 minutes, stirring often, until the mango is heated through. Add the scallions and stir to combine.

Serve over the brown rice.

NUTRITION PER SERVING: 452 calories, 49 g carbs, 5 g fiber, 42 g protein, 10 g total fat, 1 g saturated fat, 791 mg sodium

# MEDITERRANEAN TURKEY BURGERS

Recipe by MATTHEW KADEY, M.S., R.D.

**MAKES 4 SERVINGS**
**TOTAL TIME: 30 MINUTES**

### Burgers

- 1 pound lean (93%) ground turkey
- ½ cup crumbled feta cheese (2 ounces)
- ½ cup chopped roasted red bell pepper
- ⅓ cup chopped fresh basil
- ⅓ cup chopped pitted kalamata olives
- ¼ teaspoon ground black pepper
- 4 whole wheat hamburger rolls
- 1 packed cup mixed baby greens

### Sun-Dried Tomato Spread

- ½ cup julienned oil-packed sun-dried tomatoes with herbs, drained
- ⅓ cup extra-virgin olive oil
- 1 tablespoon red wine vinegar
- 1 clove garlic
- ½ teaspoon smoked paprika

*Turkey burgers are often pegged as dry and tasteless—these are anything but, thanks to the addition of moisture- and flavor-packed mix-ins. Roasted red pepper adds vitamin C, an antioxidant important for a runner's immune system. Feta cheese delivers bone-building calcium and phosphorous. Top the burgers with a sun-dried tomato spread for a dose of lycopene, a compound that may help lessen the damaging effects of the sun's UV rays and lower skin-cancer risk.*

Brush a grill rack with oil or coat a grill pan with cooking spray. Preheat the grill to medium-high heat or preheat the grill pan over medium heat.

For the burgers: In a large bowl, mix together the turkey, feta, bell pepper, basil, olives, and black pepper until thoroughly combined. Shape into 4 patties ¾ inch thick.

Grill the burgers for 6 minutes per side, or until the patties reach an internal temperature of 165°F.

Meanwhile, make the spread: In a blender or food processor, combine the sun-dried tomatoes, oil, vinegar, garlic, and smoked paprika. Blend for 1 minute, or until well combined but chunky.

Place the burgers on the rolls and serve topped with 1 tablespoon sun-dried tomato spread and the mixed baby greens.

NUTRITION PER SERVING: 463 calories, 32 g carbs, 4 g fiber, 30 g protein, 24 g total fat, 6.5 g saturated fat, 1052 mg sodium

**QUICK TIP** Any leftover sun-dried tomato spread will keep in the refrigerator for at least a month. Add to pasta, eggs, or sandwiches for a flavor boost.

# KARA GOUCHER'S KITCHEN SINK PIZZA

Recipe by KARA GOUCHER

**MAKES 4 SERVINGS**
**TOTAL TIME: 25 MINUTES**

- 4 whole wheat naan flatbreads
- ½ cup marinara sauce
- 4 teaspoons pesto
- 1 cup shredded whole-milk mozzarella cheese (4 ounces)
- 1 yellow bell pepper, chopped
- 1 cup cherry tomatoes, halved
- ¼ red onion, sliced
- ½ cup sliced mushrooms, such as cremini (about 2 ounces)
- 1 grilled chicken breast, diced
- 2 tablespoons grated Parmesan cheese
- 8 large fresh basil leaves, cut into thin ribbons

*Two-time Olympian and marathoner Kara Goucher cooks up these easy flatbread pizzas at least once a week. If you're planning to grill, set aside one grilled chicken breast (about 6 ounces cooked) to use for this recipe. Otherwise, you can use a rotisserie chicken breast.*

Preheat the oven to 400°F.

Arrange the flatbreads on 2 baking sheets. Spread a thin layer of marinara across the breads. Top each with a teaspoon of the pesto and swirl into the sauce. Sprinkle the flatbreads with the mozzarella. Top with the bell pepper, tomatoes, onion, and mushrooms. Add the chicken and finish with a sprinkle of Parmesan.

Bake the flatbreads for 12 minutes, or until the breads brown, the vegetables are softened, and the cheese melts.

Serve the pizzas garnished with the basil.

NUTRITION PER SERVING: 506 calories, 52 g carbs, 7 g fiber, 30 g protein, 19 g total fat, 7 g saturated fat, 877 mg sodium

QUICK TIP You can also substitute leftover grilled vegetables for the fresh bell pepper, tomatoes, and mushrooms.

# ORANGE-CHIPOTLE CHICKEN THIGHS

Recipe by MATTHEW KADEY, M.S., R.D.

**MAKES 4 SERVINGS**
**TOTAL TIME: 25 MINUTES**

- 2 pounds boneless, skinless chicken thighs, trimmed of excess fat
- 2 tablespoons grated orange zest
- 2 tablespoons canola oil
- 1 teaspoon chipotle powder
- ½ teaspoon ground cumin
- ½ teaspoon salt
- ½ teaspoon ground black pepper
- 1 orange, unpeeled and sliced into ¼-inch-thick rounds

*Compared to white meat, chicken thighs contain more iron and zinc—two important nutrients for runners—while broiled orange slices add a burst of juice with every bite. Serve with a side of black beans and steamed green beans.*

Position an oven rack 4 inches from the heat and preheat the broiler to high.

Arrange the chicken thighs in a broilerproof skillet or dish.

In a small bowl, combine the orange zest, oil, chipotle powder, cumin, salt, and pepper. Brush the mixture on the chicken thighs.

Place the orange slices around the chicken thighs (not on them—they will scorch). Broil for 10 to 12 minutes, until the chicken reaches an internal temperature of 165°F.

Serve each thigh with an orange slice on top.

NUTRITION PER SERVING: 354 calories, 5 g carbs, 1 g fiber, 44 g protein, 17 g total fat, 3 g saturated fat, 504 mg sodium

**QUICK TIP** Boneless chicken thighs cook a bit faster than bone-in, but you can substitute the latter if preferred. You can also use chili powder if you don't have chipotle powder.

# VIETNAMESE-STYLE PULLED CHICKEN SANDWICHES

Recipe by JENNIFER KUSHNIER

**MAKES 4 SERVINGS**
**TOTAL TIME: 20 MINUTES**

- 2 tablespoons toasted sesame oil
- 1 tablespoon fish sauce
- ½ teaspoon soy sauce
- 4 soft hoagie, Portuguese, or Cuban rolls (5 inches long), split
- ¼ red onion, cut into ¼-inch-thick rings
- ¼ cup fresh cilantro leaves
- 1½ cups shredded rotisserie chicken breast (without skin)
- 1 cup kimchi, drained
- 4 butter lettuce or Bibb lettuce leaves
- 2 tablespoons mayonnaise

*Inspired by the Vietnamese sandwich called banh mi, this pared-down version offers many of the same flavors but without the long list of ingredients typically found in many recipes. If you prefer less spice, use mild kimchi (fermented cabbage). It's packed with flavor and good-for-you probiotic bacteria. Look for it in the produce section of most grocery stores.*

Heat a large skillet over medium heat.

In a small bowl, mix together the sesame oil, fish sauce, and soy sauce and brush on the cut sides of the rolls.

Place the rolls, cut side down, in the skillet (if all 4 rolls do not fit, do this in batches). Toast for 3 minutes, or until golden and crispy.

Arrange the red onion, cilantro, chicken, kimchi, and lettuce on the bottom half of the rolls. Spread the top half of the rolls with the mayonnaise.

Close up the sandwiches and serve.

NUTRITION PER SERVING: 361 calories, 38 g carbs, 3 g fiber, 23 g protein, 11 g total fat, 2 g saturated fat, 1,084 mg sodium

**QUICK TIP** This sandwich is best with a softer roll typical of those you'd find in the packaged bread and roll aisle in most grocery stores—not in the fresh bakery section.

# GRILLED CHICKEN GYROS WITH YOGURT-CUCUMBER SAUCE

Recipe by THE RODALE TEST KITCHEN

**MAKES 4 SERVINGS**
**TOTAL TIME: 30 MINUTES**

- 4 boneless, skinless chicken breast halves (4 ounces each)
- 2 teaspoons extra-virgin olive oil
- ½ teaspoon dried oregano
- ¼ teaspoon salt
- ⅛ teaspoon ground black pepper
- ½ cup 2% plain Greek yogurt
- ½ cucumber, peeled, seeded, and chopped
- 1 small clove garlic, minced
- 4 large whole wheat pitas (6 to 8 inches)
- 1 cup chopped romaine lettuce
- ½ tomato, chopped
- ¼ red onion, thinly sliced
- ¼ cup crumbled feta cheese (1 ounce)

*Soft pita bread, crisp and crunchy vegetables, and creamy yogurt sauce make this recovery-friendly sandwich impossible to resist. You can also make it with steak or lamb, the traditional choice.*

Coat a grill pan with cooking spray and heat over medium-high heat.

In a bowl, combine the chicken, oil, oregano, salt, and pepper. Grill the chicken for 5 to 6 minutes per side, or until the thickest portion reaches an internal temperature of 165°F and the juices run clear. Transfer to a cutting board and cut into thin slices.

Meanwhile, in a small bowl, combine the yogurt, cucumber, and garlic. With the tip of a knife, cut an opening in one side of each pita.

Fill each pita with one-fourth of the romaine, tomato, onion, feta, and chicken. Spoon the yogurt-cucumber sauce over the chicken.

NUTRITION PER SERVING: 379 calories, 39 g carbs, 6 g fiber, 35 g protein, 10 g total fat, 3 g saturated fat, 682 mg sodium

**QUICK TIP** To quickly seed the cucumber, halve it lengthwise, then run the tip of a spoon down the middle. If you're really short on time, use a small English cucumber (the kind that come wrapped in plastic)—no need to peel or seed it.

# SPECIAL RECIPE LISTS

## ▶ PRERUN

Almond-Cherry Granola (page 2)

Apple Crisp Smoothie (page 40)

Auntie Oxie Juice (page 43)

"Baked" Granola Apples (page 5)

Basil-Mint Sugar Snaps (page 175)

Black Bean and Bacon Potato Salad (page 91)

Blueberries 'n' Cream Oatmeal (page 12)

Bolognese over Shells (page 150)

Bow-Ties with Roasted Cherry Tomatoes (page 142)

Bow-Ties with Tomato, Basil, and Avocado Sauce (page 128)

Broccoli with Lemon-Garlic Sauce (page 178)

Cavatappi with Peas and Prosciutto (page 143)

Chai Pumpkin Oatmeal (page 8)

Chilled Golden Zucchini and Buttermilk Soup (page 109)

Chocolate Chip Trail Mix Balls (page 55)

Coconut Shrimp with Rice Noodles (page 144)

Cranberry-Beet Smoothie (page 41)

Cucumber-Coconut Juice (page 47)

Curry Chipotle Popcorn (page 68)

Fennel Potato Salad (page 81)

Fettuccine with Ricotta-Pistachio Sauce (page 130)

Fettuccine with Spinach and Feta Sauce (page 134)

Garlic-Rosemary Pita Chips (page 66)

Gingered Winter Greens Smoothie (page 40)

Good Morning Sweet Potato (page 27)

Great Greens Juice (page 45)

Green Tea Smoothie (page 35)

Hearty Miso Soup (page 110)

High-Protein Chocolate Pudding (page 71)

Honey Energy Bars (page 50)

Honeydew Soup (page 106)

Instant Frozen Yogurt (page 71)

Island Smoothie (page 32)

Just Beet It Juice (page 44)

Lemon-Carrot Hummus (page 60)

Linguine with Green Eggs and Tomatoes (page 138)

Mashed Protein Potatoes (page 179)

Minestrone Verde (page 107)

Multigrain Buttermilk Pancake Mix (page 23)

PackFit Bars (page 51)

Penne with Broccoli Rabe and Sausage (page 149)

Power Breakfast Smoothie (page 37)

Quick-Cooking Barley and Kale Soup (page 113)

Quick-Cooking Steel-Cut Oatmeal (page 7)

Red Lentil Soup (page 112)

Roasted Balsamic Asparagus (page 179)

Roasted Curry Cauliflower (page 176)

Soba Noodles with Peanut-Sesame Sauce (page 131)

Spaghetti Carbonara (page 147)

Spaghetti with Kale and Navy Beans
(page 139)

Spaghetti with Sun-Dried Tomato Sauce
(page 133)

Spaghetti with Tuna Sauce (page 148)

Spicy Carrot Cooler (page 35)

Sporty Spice Juice (page 44)

Stir-Fry Soup (page 117)

Sunny Citrus Smoothie (page 36)

Sweet Potato Pie Smoothie (page 42)

Tomato-Basil Juice (page 45)

Tuna Caprese Pasta Salad (page 135)

Warm Gingerbread Pudding (page 72)

Warm Tomato, Olive, and Arugula Salad
(page 82)

Watermelon-Cherry Juice (page 47)

Watermelon-Mint Slushy (page 34)

## ■ RECOVERY

Asparagus and Mushroom Rice Bowl
(page 162)

Bacon-Apple-Cheddar Oatmeal (page 14)

Baked Mackerel in Spicy Tomato-
Chickpea Sauce (page 195)

Black and White Bean Sausage Soup
(page 114)

Blueberries 'n' Cream Oatmeal (page 12)

Blueberry-Walnut Pancakes with Maple
Yogurt (page 24)

Bolognese Over Shells (page 150)

Bow-Ties with Roasted Cherry Tomatoes
(page 142)

Broiled Garlicky Shrimp (page 196)

Broiled Lamb Chops with Spinach and
White Bean Sauté (page 216)

Broiled Tilapia with Mango Chutney
(page 190)

Cavatappi with Peas and Prosciutto
(page 143)

Cheesy Polenta with Caramelized
Mushrooms (page 169)

Chickpea Cherry Frittata (page 159)

Chipotle-Cocoa Bison Burgers
(page 212)

Chocolate-Banana Granola Bowls
(page 6)

Chunky Tomato-Beef Soup (page 120)

Coconut Mahi-Mahi with Pineapple Salsa
(page 189)

Coconut Shrimp with Rice Noodles
(page 144)

Couscous with White Beans and Roasted
Red Pepper (page 160)

Creamy Fish Chowder (page 125)

Curry Crab Burgers (page 199)

"Eggy" Tofu Scramble (page 15)

Fettuccine with Ricotta-Pistachio Sauce
(page 130)

Fettuccine with Spinach and Feta Sauce
(page 134)

Gazpacho Chicken Salad (page 89)

Gingered Beef with Broccolini and
Cashews (page 207)

Green and White Bean Salad with Tuna
(page 98)

Green Eggs and Ham Oatmeal (page 9)

Grilled Chicken Gyros with Yogurt-
Cucumber Sauce (page 229)

Halibut with Lemon-Caper Sauce
(page 183)

Honey-Soy Glazed Arctic Char (page 188)

Indian-Spiced Boneless Pork Chops
(page 214)

Kara Goucher's Kitchen Sink Pizza
(page 222)

## ▶ VEGETARIAN

Blueberry-Walnut Pancakes with Maple Yogurt (page 24)

Bow-Ties with Tomato, Basil, and Avocado Sauce (page 128)

Broccoli with Lemon-Garlic Sauce (page 178)

Chai Pumpkin Oatmeal (page 8)

Cheesy Polenta with Caramelized Mushrooms (page 169)

Chickpea Cherry Frittata (page 159)

Chilled Golden Zucchini and Buttermilk Soup (page 109)

Chocolate Avocado Spread (page 61)

Chocolate-Banana Granola Bowls (page 6)

Chocolate Chip Trail Mix Balls (page 55)

Couscous with White Beans and Roasted Red Pepper (page 160)

Cranberry-Beet Smoothie (page 41)

Creamy Avocado Dressing (page 99)

Cucumber-Coconut Juice (page 47)

Curried Pumpkin Soup (page 118)

Curry Chipotle Popcorn (page 68)

Date Balls (page 56)

Dijon Lemon Vinaigrette (page 99)

Edamame-Basil Dip (page 58)

"Eggy" Tofu Scramble (page 15)

El Guapo's Great Energy Bars (page 52)

Fennel Potato Salad (page 81)

Fettuccine with Ricotta-Pistachio Sauce (page 130)

Fettuccine with Spinach and Feta Sauce (page 134)

Figs with Mascarpone and Honey (page 72)

Fresh Herb Vinaigrette (page 101)

Garlic-Rosemary Pita Chips (page 66)

Gingered Winter Greens Smoothie (page 40)

Good Morning Sweet Potato (page 27)

Great Greens Juice (page 45)

Green Tea Smoothie (page 35)

Grilled Eggplant and Fresh Mozzarella Sandwiches (page 161)

Hearty Miso Soup (page 110)

High-Protein Chocolate Pudding (page 71)

Honey Energy Bars (page 50)

Honeydew Soup (page 106)

Instant Frozen Yogurt (page 71)

Island Smoothie (page 32)

Jicama Slaw (page 80)

Just Beet It Juice (page 44)

Lemon-Carrot Hummus (page 60)

Linguine with Green Eggs and Tomatoes (page 138)

Liz's Famous Guacamole (page 57)

Loaded Bruschetta (page 171)

Make-Ahead Tomato Sauce (page 156)

Maple-Cinnamon Walnut Butter (page 62)

Mashed Protein Potatoes (page 179)

Minestrone Verde (page 107)

Mocha Madness Recovery Shake (page 37)

Multigrain Buttermilk Pancake Mix (page 23)

PackFit Bars (page 51)

Pizza Margherita with Make-Ahead Tomato Sauce (page 154)

Power Breakfast Smoothie (page 37)

Pumpkin-Ricotta Waffles (page 22)

Quick Blueberry Sauce (page 26)

Quick-Cooking Steel-Cut Oatmeal (page 7)

Quinoa-Kale Salad with Fresh Apricots (page 96)

Red Lentil Soup (page 112)

Roasted Balsamic Asparagus (page 179)

Roasted Curry Cauliflower (page 176)

Sautéed Baby Kale and Pine Nuts
(page 172)

Sesame-Almond Mix (page 67)

Simple (or Stuffed!) Omelets (page 16)

Smoky Black Bean Stew (page 119)

Smoky Squash Flatbread with Balsamic
Glaze (page 157)

Smoky Sriracha Peanut Butter (page 62)

Soba Noodles with Peanut-Sesame Sauce
(page 131)

Southwestern Black Bean Wrap (page 21)

Spaghetti with Kale and Navy Beans
(page 139)

Spiced Chickpeas with Spinach (page 166)

Spicy Carrot Cooler (page 35)

Spicy Miso Dressing (page 101)

Sporty Spice Juice (page 44)

Spring Lettuces with Strawberries and
Feta (page 86)

Spring Run Smoothie (page 33)

Stir-Fry Soup (page 117)

Strawberry-Pistachio Pita Pizzas
(page 29)

Sunny Citrus Smoothie (page 36)

Super "Cheesy" Kale Chips (page 65)

Sweet and Salty Pistachio Butter
(page 64)

Sweet Potato Pie Smoothie (page 42)

Sweet Potato–Black Bean Falafel
(page 165)

Sweet Potato–Pumpkin Seed Salad
(page 85)

Tahini and Sun-Dried Tomato Dip
(page 58)

Tofu Peanut Stir-Fry (page 170)

Tomato-Basil Juice (page 45)

Tropical Twister Oatmeal (page 13)

Warm Gingerbread Pudding (page 72)

Warm Tomato, Olive, and Arugula Salad
(page 82)

Watermelon-Cherry Juice (page 47)

Watermelon-Mint Slushy (page 34)

Whole Grain Panzanella (page 79)

## ◗ VEGAN

Almond-Cherry Granola (page 2)

Auntie Oxie Juice (page 43)

Basil-Mint Sugar Snaps (page 175)

Bow-Ties with Tomato, Basil, and Avocado
Sauce (page 128)

Broccoli with Lemon-Garlic Sauce
(page 178)

Chocolate Chip Trail Mix Balls (page 55)

Cranberry-Beet Smoothie (page 41)

Creamy Avocado Dressing (page 99)

Cucumber-Coconut Juice (page 47)

Curry Chipotle Popcorn (page 68)

Date Balls (page 56)

Dijon Lemon Vinaigrette (page 99)

Edamame-Basil Dip (page 58)

"Eggy" Tofu Scramble (page 15)

El Guapo's Great Energy Bars (page 52)

Fresh Herb Vinaigrette (page 101)

Garlic-Rosemary Pita Chips (page 66)

Good Morning Sweet Potato (page 27)

Great Greens Juice (page 45)

Green Tea Smoothie (page 35)

Hearty Miso Soup (page 110)

High-Protein Chocolate Pudding
(page 71)

Just Beet It Juice (page 44)

Liz's Famous Guacamole (page 57)

Loaded Bruschetta (page 171)

Make-Ahead Tomato Sauce (page 156)

Maple-Cinnamon Walnut Butter
(page 62)

Quick-Cooking Steel-Cut Oatmeal
(page 7)

Red Lentil Soup (page 112)

Roasted Balsamic Asparagus
(page 179)

Roasted Curry Cauliflower (page 176)

Sautéed Baby Kale and Pine Nuts
(page 172)

Smoky Black Bean Stew (page 119)

Smoky Sriracha Peanut Butter
(page 62)

Soba Noodles with Peanut-Sesame Sauce
(page 131)

Spicy Carrot Cooler (page 35)

Sporty Spice Juice (page 44)

Spring Run Smoothie (page 33)

Stir-Fry Soup (page 117)

Strawberry-Pistachio Pita Pizzas
(page 29)

Super "Cheesy" Kale Chips (page 65)

Sweet Potato–Black Bean Falafel
(page 165)

Sweet Potato Pie Smoothie (page 42)

Tahini and Sun-Dried Tomato Dip
(page 58)

Tofu Peanut Stir-Fry (page 170)

Tomato-Basil Juice (page 45)

Tropical Twister Oatmeal (page 13)

Warm Gingerbread Pudding (page 72)

Watermelon-Cherry Juice (page 47)

Watermelon-Mint Slushy (page 34)

Whole Grain Panzanella (page 79)

## ▌ LOW-CALORIE

Almond-Cherry Granola (page 2)

Almond-Coconut Butter (page 64)

Apple Crisp Smoothie (page 40)

Auntie Oxie Juice (page 43)

"Baked" Granola Apples (page 5)

Basil-Mint Sugar Snaps (page 175)

Black and White Bean Sausage Soup
(page 114)

Black Bean and Bacon Potato Salad
(page 91)

Blueberries 'n' Cream Oatmeal
(page 12)

Broccoli with Lemon-Garlic Sauce
(page 178)

Broiled Garlicky Shrimp (page 196)

Broiled Lamb Chops with Spinach and
White Bean Sauté (page 216)

Broiled Tilapia with Mango Chutney
(page 190)

Chai Pumpkin Oatmeal (page 8)

Chickpea Cherry Frittata (page 159)

Chilled Golden Zucchini and Buttermilk
Soup (page 109)

Chocolate Avocado Spread (page 61)

Chocolate Chip Trail Mix Balls
(page 55)

Chunky Tomato-Beef Soup (page 120)

Coconut Mahi-Mahi with Pineapple Salsa
(page 189)

Cold Avocado and Crab Soup (page 104)

Cranberry-Beet Smoothie (page 41)

Creamy Avocado Dressing (page 99)

Creamy Fish Chowder (page 125)

Cucumber-Coconut Juice (page 47)

Shortcut Thai Beef Salad (page 90)

Simple (or Stuffed!) Omelets (page 16)

Smoked Salmon Pizza (page 187)

Smoky Black Bean Stew (page 119)

Smoky Sriracha Peanut Butter (page 62)

Soba Noodles with Peanut-Sesame Sauce
(page 131)

Spice-Rubbed Flank Steak with
Chile-Tomato Salsa (page 206)

Spiced Chickpeas with Spinach (page 166)

Spicy Carrot Cooler (page 35)

Spicy Miso Dressing (page 101)

Spicy Salmon and Rice Noodle Soup
(page 123)

Sporty Spice Juice (page 44)

Spring Lettuces with Strawberries and
Feta (page 86)

Spring Run Smoothie (page 33)

Stir-Fried Tofu and Shrimp (page 198)

Stir-Fry Soup (page 117)

Strawberry-Pistachio Pita Pizzas
(page 29)

Summer Corn Salad (page 76)

Sunny Citrus Smoothie (page 36)

Super "Cheesy" Kale Chips (page 65)

Sweet and Salty Pistachio Butter
(page 64)

Sweet Potato Chicken Stew (page 124)

Sweet Potato Pie Smoothie (page 42)

Sweet Potato–Pumpkin Seed Salad
(page 85)

Tahini and Sun-Dried Tomato Dip
(page 58)

Thai Fish Curry (page 184)

Tomato-Basil Juice (page 45)

Tropical Twister Oatmeal (page 13)

Vietnamese-Style Pulled Chicken
Sandwiches (page 226)

Warm Gingerbread Pudding (page 72)

Warm Tomato, Olive, and Arugula
Salad (page 82)

Watermelon-Cherry Juice (page 47)

Watermelon-Mint Slushy (page 34)

Whole Grain Panzanella (page 79)

## ▌ GLUTEN-FREE

Almond-Coconut Butter (page 64)

Apple Crisp Smoothie (page 40)

Asparagus and Mushroom Rice Bowl
(page 162)

Auntie Oxie Juice (page 43)

Bacon-Apple-Cheddar Oatmeal (page 14)

Baked Mackerel in Spicy Tomato-
Chickpea Sauce (page 195)

Basil-Mint Sugar Snaps (page 175)

Black and White Bean Sausage Soup
(page 114)

Black Bean and Bacon Potato Salad
(page 91)

Blueberries 'n' Cream Oatmeal (page 12)

Broccoli with Lemon-Garlic Sauce
(page 178)

Broiled Garlicky Shrimp (page 196)

Broiled Lamb Chops with Spinach and
White Bean Sauté (page 216)

Broiled Tilapia with Mango Chutney
(page 190)

Chai Pumpkin Oatmeal (page 8)

Cheesy Polenta with Caramelized
Mushrooms (page 169)

Chickpea Cherry Frittata (page 159)

Chilled Golden Zucchini and Buttermilk
Soup (page 109)

Chocolate Avocado Spread (page 61)

Sweet Potato Chicken Stew (page 124)

Sweet Potato Pie Smoothie (page 42)

Sweet Potato–Pumpkin Seed Salad
(page 85)

Tahini and Sun-Dried Tomato Dip
(page 58)

Thai Fish Curry (page 184)

Tomato-Basil Juice (page 45)

Tropical Twister Oatmeal (page 13)

Warm Gingerbread Pudding (page 72)

Warm Tomato, Olive, and Arugula Salad
(page 82)

Watermelon-Cherry Juice (page 47)

Watermelon-Mint Slushy (page 34)

## ▶ 5-MINUTE FIX

Auntie Oxie Juice (page 43)

Creamy Avocado Dressing (page 99)

Curry Chipotle Popcorn (page 68)

Dijon Lemon Vinaigrette (page 99)

Fresh Herb Vinaigrette (page 101)

High-Protein Chocolate Pudding
(page 71)

Instant Frozen Yogurt (page 71)

Maple-Cinnamon Walnut Butter
(page 62)

Pumpkin-Ricotta Waffles (page 22)

Quick Blueberry Sauce (page 26)

Smoky Sriracha Peanut Butter (page 62)

Sweet and Salty Pistachio Butter
(page 64)

Tomato-Basil Juice (page 45)

Watermelon-Cherry Juice (page 47)

## ▶ 10 MINUTES TOPS

Almond-Coconut Butter (page 64)

Apple Crisp Smoothie (page 40)

"Baked" Granola Apples (page 5)

Chilled Golden Zucchini and Buttermilk
Soup (page 109)

Chocolate Avocado Spread (page 61)

Chocolate-Banana Granola Bowls
(page 6)

Cranberry-Beet Smoothie (page 41)

Cucumber-Coconut Juice (page 47)

Figs with Mascarpone and Honey
(page 72)

Gingered Winter Greens Smoothie
(page 40)

Great Greens Juice (page 45)

Green Tea Smoothie (page 35)

Honeydew Soup (page 106)

Island Smoothie (page 32)

Jicama Slaw (page 80)

Just Beet It Juice (page 44)

Liz's Famous Guacamole (page 57)

Mocha Madness Recovery Shake
(page 37)

Multigrain Buttermilk Pancake Mix
(page 23)

Power Breakfast Smoothie (page 37)

Sautéed Baby Kale and Pine Nuts
(page 172)

Shortcut Thai Beef Salad (page 90)

Simple (or Stuffed!) Omelets (page 16)

Spicy Carrot Cooler (page 35)

Spicy Miso Dressing (page 101)

## ▶ HYDRATING

# RECIPE CONTRIBUTORS

We thank these food writers, recipe developers, chefs, nutritionists, and elite runners, whose recipes appear in this book.

## Pam Anderson

Bow-Ties with Tomato, Basil, and Avocado Sauce (page 128)

Green and White Bean Salad with Tuna (page 98)

Quinoa-Kale Salad with Fresh Apricots (page 96)

Spaghetti with Tuna Sauce (page 148)

## Liz Applegate, Ph.D.

Black and White Bean Sausage Soup (page 114)

Chocolate Avocado Spread (page 61)

Fennel Potato Salad (page 81)

Honey Energy Bars (page 50)

Liz's Famous Guacamole (page 57)

Mashed Protein Potatoes (page 179)

Mocha Madness Recovery Shake (page 37)

## Nate Appleman

Cavatappi with Peas and Prosciutto (page 143)

Power Breakfast Smoothie (page 37)

Quick Blueberry Sauce (page 26)

Spaghetti with Sun-Dried Tomato Sauce (page 133)

Tahini and Sun-Dried Tomato Dip (page 58)

## Will Artley

PackFit Bars (page 51)

## Mark Bittman

Good Morning Sweet Potato (page 27)

Hearty Miso Soup (page 110)

Skillet Hoppin' John (page 219)

Stir-Fried Tofu and Shrimp (page 198)

Strawberry-Pistachio Pita Pizzas (page 29)

Sweet Potato–Pumpkin Seed Salad (page 85)

## Leslie Bonci, M.P.H., R.D., C.S.S.D., L.D.N.

Cucumber-Coconut Juice (page 47)

Watermelon-Cherry Juice (page 47)

## Cherie Calbom, M.S., C.N.

Tomato-Basil Juice (page 45)

## Joe Cross

Auntie Oxie Juice (page 43)

Great Greens Juice (page 45)

Just Beet It Juice (page 44)

Sporty Spice Juice (page 44)

## Amy Fritch

Date Balls (page 56)

"Eggy" Tofu Scramble (page 15)

Honeydew Soup (page 106)

## Joanna Sayago Golub

Chocolate Chip Trail Mix Balls (page 55)

Chunky Tomato-Beef Soup (page 120)

Garlic-Rosemary Pita Chips (page 66)

Green Tea Smoothie (page 35)

Loaded Bruschetta (page 171)

Red Lentil Soup (page 112)

Roasted Balsamic Asparagus (page 179)

Roasted Curry Cauliflower (page 176)

Spaghetti Carbonara (page 147)

Spring Run Smoothie (page 33)

Stir-Fry Soup (page 117)

Sweet Potato Chicken Stew (page 124)

## Amy Gorin

Pumpkin-Ricotta Waffles (page 22)

Southwestern Black Bean Wrap (page 21)

## Kara Goucher

Kara Goucher's Kitchen Sink Pizza (page 222)

## Matthew Kadey, M.S., R.D.

Apple Crisp Smoothie (page 40)

Asparagus and Mushroom Rice Bowl (page 162)

Bacon-Apple-Cheddar Oatmeal (page 14)

Blueberries 'n' Cream Oatmeal (page 12)

Chai Pumpkin Oatmeal (page 8)

Chipotle-Cocoa Bison Burgers (page 212)

Chocolate-Banana Granola Bowls (page 6)

Coconut Shrimp with Rice Noodles (page 144)

Cold Avocado and Crab Soup (page 104)

Cranberry-Beet Smoothie (page 41)

Curry Crab Burgers (page 199)

Gazpacho Chicken Salad (page 89)

Gingered Winter Greens Smoothie (page 40)

Green Eggs and Ham Oatmeal (page 9)

Jicama Slaw (page 80)

Lettuce-Wrapped Asian Salmon Burgers (page 193)

Linguine with Green Eggs and Tomatoes (page 138)

Make-Ahead Tomato Sauce (page 156)

Mediterranean Chicken and Penne (page 136)

Mediterranean Turkey Burgers (page 221)

Orange-Chipotle Chicken Thighs (page 225)

Pizza Margherita with Make-Ahead Tomato Sauce (page 154)

Quick-Cooking Steel-Cut Oatmeal (page 7)

Rotini with Pears and Prosciutto (page 141)

Salmon Cups with Avocado Sauce (page 194)

Shrimp and Asparagus Salad with Carrot Dressing (page 95)

Smoky Black Bean Stew (page 119)

Spaghetti with Kale and Navy Beans (page 139)

Steak and Peach Salad (page 92)

Steak and Pepper Rice Bowl (page 211)

Sunny Side Up Pizza (page 218)

Sweet and Spicy Chicken Stir-Fry (page 220)

Sweet Potato Pie Smoothie (page 42)

Sweet Potato–Black Bean Falafel (page 165)

Tropical Twister Oatmeal (page 13)

Tuna Caprese Pasta Salad (page 135)

Warm Gingerbread Pudding (page 72)

Watermelon-Mint Slushy (page 34)

## Matthew Kadey, M.S., R.D., and the Rodale Test Kitchen

Smoky Squash Flatbread with Balsamic Glaze (page 157)

## Ilana Katz, M.S., R.D., C.S.S.D.

Spicy Carrot Cooler (page 35)

## Jennifer Kushnier

Cheesy Polenta with Caramelized Mushrooms (page 169)

Creamy Fish Chowder (page 125)

Instant Frozen Yogurt (page 71)

Smoked Salmon Pizza (page 187)

Super "Cheesy" Kale Chips (page 65)

Vietnamese-Style Pulled Chicken Sandwiches (page 226)

## Melissa Lasher

Black Bean and Bacon Potato Salad (page 91)

Blueberry-Walnut Pancakes with Maple Yogurt (page 24)

Bow-Ties with Roasted Cherry Tomatoes (page 142)

Shortcut Thai Beef Salad (page 90)

## Bill Lynch

El Guapo's Great Energy Bars (page 52)

## Jessica Migala

Almond-Coconut Butter (page 64)

Maple-Cinnamon Walnut Butter (page 62)

Smoky Sriracha Peanut Butter (page 62)

Sweet and Salty Pistachio Butter (page 64)

## Frances Price, R.D.

Fettuccine with Spinach and Feta Sauce (page 134)

## Rodale Test Kitchen

Almond-Cherry Granola (page 2)

"Baked" Granola Apples (page 5)

Baked Mackerel in Spicy Tomato-Chickpea Sauce (page 195)

Basil-Mint Sugar Snaps (page 175)

Bolognese Over Shells (page 150)

Broccoli with Lemon-Garlic Sauce (page 178)

Broiled Garlicky Shrimp (page 196)

Broiled Lamb Chops with Spinach and White Bean Sauté (page 216)

Broiled Tilapia with Mango Chutney (page 190)

Coconut Mahi-Mahi with Pineapple Salsa (page 189)

Couscous with White Beans and Roasted Red Pepper (page 160)

Creamy Avocado Dressing (page 99)

Curried Pumpkin Soup (page 118)

Dijon Lemon Vinaigrette (page 99)

Edamame-Basil Dip (page 58)

Fettuccine with Ricotta-Pistachio Sauce (page 130)

Figs with Mascarpone and Honey (page 72)

Fresh Herb Vinaigrette (page 101)

Gingered Beef with Broccolini and Cashews (page 207)

Grilled Chicken Gyros with Yogurt-Cucumber Sauce (page 229)

Grilled Eggplant and Fresh Mozzarella Sandwiches (page 161)

Halibut with Lemon-Caper Sauce (page 183)

Honey-Soy Glazed Arctic Char (page 188)

Indian-Spiced Boneless Pork Chops (page 214)

Island Smoothie (page 32)

## Sam Talbot

## Rachel Meltzer Warren, M.S., R.D.

## Patricia Wells

## Claudia Wilson, M.S., R.D., C.S.S.D., C.S.C.S.

# ACKNOWLEDGMENTS

A huge amount of gratitude goes out to all the people (and there are many of them) who made this cookbook possible. Without each of their contributions, this beautifully designed, perfectly photographed, and meticulously tested and edited book would not be the amazing resource it is.

Thank you first to the recipe contributors and to the Rodale Test Kitchen team—JoAnn Brader, Jennifer Kushnier, and Amy Fritch. This small but mighty team put every recipe through the ringer until it was amazingly delicious and reliable. Expert sports dietitian Pamela Nisevich Bede, M.S., R.D., C.S.S.D., L.D., weighed in on the recipes, as well, to ensure they offered runners true performance benefits.

I'd like to thank my editor Mark Weinstein, who helped shepherd this project along from the very start, and senior project editor Nancy N. Bailey, whose expertise touches every page. Thank you to art director Christina Gaugler, photographer Mitch Mandel, and stylists Adrienne Anderson and Paige Hicks—their amazing collaboration is evident in the gorgeous design and photography throughout the book.

Finally, I'd like to thank the readers of *Runner's World* and all those who enjoyed (and continue to enjoy) our first project, *The Runner's World Cookbook*. Without the loyal and inspiring community of runners, books like this one would not be possible.

—*Joanna Sayago Golub*

# ABOUT THE EDITOR

The former longtime nutrition editor at *Runner's World* magazine, Joanna Sayago Golub is a freelance food and nutrition writer and editor. She lives and runs in Bethlehem, Pennsylvania.

# INDEX

Underscored page references indicate boxed text. **Boldface** references indicate photographs.